CI/CD WITH AZURE

Build Pipelines Like a Pro

FIRST EDITION

Preface

In the ever-evolving landscape of software development, the need for faster, more reliable, and scalable delivery mechanisms has never been more pressing. Continuous Integration and Continuous Delivery (CI/CD) practices have become the cornerstone of modern software engineering, enabling teams to deliver value rapidly while maintaining high quality and security standards. This book, *CI/CD with Azure: Build Pipelines Like a Pro*, is designed to demystify CI/CD processes and provide a hands-on introduction to building and managing modern DevOps pipelines using Azure DevOps.

Whether you're a software developer, DevOps engineer, QA professional, or IT manager, this book will help you understand the principles of CI/CD, explore Azure DevOps capabilities, and implement end-to-end pipeline solutions tailored to real-world applications.

We begin by exploring the foundational concepts of CI/CD and the evolution of software delivery practices. From there, we dive into the practical aspects of setting up and managing Azure DevOps environments, followed by an in-depth look at YAML-based pipelines and automation.

Subsequent chapters address advanced CI strategies, deployment techniques, security considerations, monitoring, and real-world case studies to solidify your understanding. In the final chapter, we cast an eye to the future, covering emerging tools, trends, and how DevOps continues to shape software engineering.

Each chapter builds on the previous one, ensuring a cohesive learning experience with clear, actionable guidance. You'll find step-by-step examples, configuration advice, and best practices distilled from years of industry experience.

Whether you are just starting out or looking to deepen your understanding of Azure DevOps, this book is your practical companion in mastering CI/CD with confidence.

Table of Contents

Chapter 1: Introduction to CI/CD and Azure DevOps

The Evolution of Software Delivery

The way we build, test, and deliver software has transformed dramatically over the past few decades. Traditionally, software development followed a waterfall approach—rigid, sequential stages that often resulted in slow releases, poor adaptability, and increased risk of failure. Projects would span months or even years, with limited opportunities for customer feedback until the very end. This led to a growing recognition of the need for more agile and responsive delivery models.

The advent of Agile methodologies marked a turning point in software development. Agile introduced iterative development, faster feedback loops, and collaboration between cross-functional teams. This shift in mindset paved the way for the emergence of DevOps, a culture and practice aimed at unifying development and operations teams to streamline the delivery pipeline.

DevOps is not merely a set of tools—it's a cultural shift focused on collaboration, automation, and continuous improvement. With DevOps came the concepts of Continuous Integration (CI) and Continuous Delivery/Deployment (CD), which have since become the backbone of modern software engineering.

Continuous Integration (CI) is the practice of automatically integrating code changes into a shared repository several times a day. This process ensures that changes are tested frequently, reducing integration issues and identifying bugs early in the development cycle.

Continuous Delivery (CD) builds upon CI by ensuring that software can be reliably released to production at any time. The final step—**Continuous Deployment**—goes a step further by automatically deploying every successful build to production without manual intervention.

These practices have revolutionized software delivery, enabling teams to release new features, fixes, and updates at unprecedented speed and scale.

The Rise of DevOps Toolchains

As CI/CD gained traction, a multitude of tools emerged to support each aspect of the pipeline. Tools like Jenkins, Travis CI, CircleCI, and GitLab CI became popular for building and testing code. However, many organizations struggled with integrating these tools into a cohesive workflow that could scale across teams and projects.

This is where **Azure DevOps** enters the picture.

Microsoft's Azure DevOps offers an end-to-end suite of tools for planning, developing, building, testing, and delivering software. Unlike fragmented toolchains, Azure DevOps provides a unified platform that integrates seamlessly with Azure cloud services and other third-party tools. Whether you're deploying to virtual machines, Kubernetes clusters, or Azure App Services, Azure DevOps simplifies the process with powerful automation and collaboration features.

Azure DevOps includes:

- **Azure Repos** for source control using Git or Team Foundation Version Control (TFVC).

- **Azure Pipelines** for building and deploying code automatically.

- **Azure Boards** for tracking work using Agile methodologies.

- **Azure Artifacts** for managing packages.

- **Azure Test Plans** for managing test cases and automated testing.

With Azure DevOps, teams can adopt CI/CD practices with minimal setup and maximum flexibility, making it an ideal platform for both startups and enterprise environments.

The Shift Toward Infrastructure as Code

Another key advancement influencing modern software delivery is **Infrastructure as Code (IaC)**. Traditionally, infrastructure provisioning was a manual process, often leading to inconsistent environments and configuration drift. IaC changes this by allowing infrastructure to be defined in code, version-controlled, and deployed using the same CI/CD pipelines used for application code.

Azure DevOps integrates well with tools like Terraform, ARM templates, and Bicep, allowing you to define and deploy infrastructure alongside your application code. This unification further enhances the reliability, repeatability, and traceability of deployments.

Benefits of Adopting CI/CD and Azure DevOps

Organizations that embrace CI/CD practices through platforms like Azure DevOps report significant benefits:

- **Faster Time-to-Market**: Automated pipelines reduce the time between writing code and deploying it to production.

- **Improved Quality**: Frequent testing and feedback loops result in higher code quality and fewer bugs in production.

- **Enhanced Collaboration**: Developers, testers, and operations teams work together in a shared environment.

- **Increased Efficiency**: Automation reduces manual tasks, freeing up teams to focus on innovation.

- **Greater Confidence**: Every change is tested and validated through repeatable processes, making deployments less risky.

The adoption of CI/CD is no longer optional in today's fast-paced development landscape—it's essential.

The Human Side of DevOps

While tools and automation are critical, the success of DevOps hinges on people. A true DevOps culture promotes shared responsibility, continuous learning, and open communication. Teams must break down silos, embrace feedback, and iterate constantly to improve both processes and outcomes.

Azure DevOps fosters this culture by providing shared tools that support visibility, traceability, and collaboration. Dashboards, notifications, and integrations ensure everyone stays informed and aligned throughout the development lifecycle.

A Glimpse Ahead

This chapter set the stage for everything that follows. We've looked at how software delivery has evolved, the core concepts of CI/CD, and how Azure DevOps supports modern development practices.

In the next chapters, we'll roll up our sleeves and begin setting up your Azure DevOps environment, managing projects, configuring permissions, and connecting to your favorite tools and services.

Here's a quick preview of what's coming:

- Learn how to create an Azure DevOps organization and navigate its interface.

- Explore pipeline creation using YAML.

- Automate builds, tests, and deployments.

- Implement security, auditing, and monitoring practices.

- Analyze real-world use cases and prepare for the future of DevOps.

Whether you're building your first CI/CD pipeline or scaling DevOps across your enterprise, the journey starts now—with a clear understanding of the foundations. Let's begin.

CI/CD Principles and Benefits

Continuous Integration and Continuous Delivery/Deployment (CI/CD) are at the heart of modern software engineering practices. Together, they represent a set of operating principles and a collection of practices that enable development teams to deliver code changes more frequently, reliably, and efficiently. Understanding the core principles of CI/CD not only provides a foundation for adopting DevOps practices but also helps teams establish a culture of high performance and collaboration.

Understanding Continuous Integration (CI)

Continuous Integration refers to the practice of frequently merging all developer working copies to a shared mainline (often multiple times a day). The primary goal is to detect integration issues early and fix them rapidly.

Key principles of CI:

- **Automated Builds**: Every commit triggers an automated build, ensuring that code compiles and basic operations work as expected.

- **Automated Tests**: Builds run automated unit and integration tests to validate functionality.

- **Version Control Integration**: CI tools integrate tightly with Git or other version control systems, monitoring repositories for changes.

- **Fast Feedback Loops**: Developers are notified immediately if a build or test fails, allowing them to fix issues promptly.

Sample YAML CI Pipeline in Azure DevOps:

```
trigger:
  branches:
    include:
      - main

pool:
  vmImage: 'ubuntu-latest'

steps:
- task: UseDotNet@2
  inputs:
    packageType: 'sdk'
    version: '6.x.x'

- script: dotnet build
  displayName: 'Build Project'
```

```
- script: dotnet test
  displayName: 'Run Tests'
```

In the example above, every change pushed to the `main` branch triggers a build, compiles the project, and runs tests using .NET.

Understanding Continuous Delivery and Deployment

Whereas CI focuses on code integration and testing, **Continuous Delivery (CD)** ensures that the software is always in a deployable state. It involves deploying every build to a staging environment and preparing it for production with minimal manual intervention.

Continuous Deployment, often used interchangeably with Continuous Delivery, goes one step further by automatically deploying every change that passes all pipeline stages directly to production.

Key principles of CD:

- **Automated Releases**: Builds are deployed automatically through environments—development, staging, and production.

- **Configuration Management**: Environment-specific settings are managed via configuration files or secrets management.

- **Approval Gates**: Optional manual or automated gates are included before production deployment.

- **Rollback Mechanisms**: Failed deployments can be rolled back to a previous stable state.

Release Pipeline Configuration Snippet:

```
stages:
- stage: DeployStaging
  jobs:
  - deployment: DeployWebApp
    environment: staging
    strategy:
      runOnce:
        deploy:
          steps:
          - task: AzureWebApp@1
            inputs:
```

```
appName: 'my-app-staging'
package: '$(System.DefaultWorkingDirectory)/**/*.zip'
```

The above configuration defines a deployment stage targeting a staging environment using the AzureWebApp task.

Core CI/CD Practices

A successful CI/CD pipeline is underpinned by several best practices and patterns:

1. Commit Early, Commit Often

Frequent commits allow smaller, incremental changes to be tested and integrated, reducing the risk of conflicts and regressions.

2. Test Automation

Tests are the safety net of CI/CD. Unit, integration, and end-to-end tests must be included and maintained. As the codebase grows, so must the test suite.

3. Build Once, Deploy Many

Artifacts should be created once during the CI process and reused across environments in the CD pipeline. This ensures consistency and avoids environment-specific issues.

4. Fail Fast

CI/CD systems should fail fast—if a build or test fails, it should be immediately visible. Broken pipelines must be fixed before any new changes are accepted.

5. Pipeline as Code

Storing pipeline definitions in version control enables collaboration, history tracking, and better governance.

6. Incremental Deployments

Deployments should be incremental, preferably using techniques like blue/green or canary releases to mitigate risk.

Benefits of CI/CD

The benefits of CI/CD extend far beyond automation. They fundamentally change how teams develop, release, and support software.

Accelerated Development and Release Cycles

CI/CD reduces the cycle time between idea and delivery. Teams can deploy changes to users more quickly, respond to feedback faster, and continuously improve their product.

This acceleration is especially crucial in competitive industries where time-to-market can be a differentiator.

Improved Code Quality and Reliability

By integrating testing and validation early in the development process, CI/CD detects issues sooner. Automated builds and tests ensure consistent behavior and eliminate many of the errors traditionally caught late in the cycle.

Reduced Integration Risk

Integration issues that used to take days or weeks to resolve are now addressed within minutes. Since developers are merging their changes frequently, conflicts are minimized, and when they do occur, they're easier to resolve.

Enhanced Developer Productivity

CI/CD reduces the burden of manual testing, deployment scripting, and release coordination. Developers can focus on writing features instead of managing releases.

Additionally, fast feedback on changes encourages a culture of experimentation and iteration.

Easier Rollbacks and Disaster Recovery

With proper artifact and version management, teams can easily roll back to a previous version in case of issues. This enhances system resilience and supports high availability.

Azure DevOps supports artifact storage, deployment logs, and approval workflows that make rollbacks straightforward.

Better Collaboration Across Teams

CI/CD creates shared ownership of quality and delivery. Developers, testers, and operations personnel collaborate more closely, often using the same dashboards, logs, and deployment histories.

Azure Boards, Pipelines, and Repos foster this collaboration by integrating work items, code, and builds under a unified interface.

Metrics and Insights for Improvement

CI/CD systems provide rich telemetry: build times, success rates, test coverage, deployment durations, and more. These metrics help identify bottlenecks and guide continuous improvement.

Teams can use Azure DevOps Analytics or integrate with Azure Monitor, Application Insights, and other observability platforms to gain even deeper insight into pipeline health.

Culture Change and CI/CD

While the technical benefits of CI/CD are numerous, adopting it often requires a significant cultural transformation:

- **From Siloes to Collaboration**: Development, QA, and Ops must break down barriers and work in integrated teams.

- **From Manual to Automated**: Teams must invest in scripting, tooling, and automation frameworks.

- **From Fear of Change to Embracing Change**: Frequent deployments shift risk management from avoidance to containment.

- **From Big Bang Releases to Incremental Delivery**: The release cadence changes from quarterly or monthly to daily or hourly.

These shifts are not always easy, but they are necessary to realize the full value of CI/CD.

CI/CD Anti-Patterns to Avoid

As important as best practices are, it's also critical to recognize and avoid common pitfalls:

- **"One-Time Setup" Mentality**: Pipelines should evolve with your code and workflows.

- **Excessive Manual Gates**: These slow down delivery and often replicate what automation should do.

- **Lack of Test Coverage**: CI/CD is only as effective as the tests that run within it.

- **Poor Secret Management**: Storing passwords or tokens in pipeline code is a serious security risk.

- **Ignoring Pipeline Failures**: A red build should be treated as a top priority—never ignored.

Measuring CI/CD Success

To gauge the effectiveness of your CI/CD implementation, consider the following key performance indicators (KPIs):

- **Lead Time for Changes**: Time from commit to production.

- **Deployment Frequency**: How often code is released to production.

- **Change Failure Rate**: Percentage of deployments that cause incidents.

- **Mean Time to Recovery (MTTR)**: How long it takes to recover from a failure.

These metrics—popularized by the DORA research program—are now industry standards for evaluating DevOps performance.

Conclusion

CI/CD represents not just a technical shift, but a fundamental evolution in how software is built and delivered. The principles outlined in this section—automation, fast feedback, frequent integration, and safe deployment—form the backbone of a high-performing DevOps culture.

By embracing these principles and applying them through tools like Azure DevOps, organizations can achieve faster delivery, better quality, and a more collaborative engineering environment. The journey toward CI/CD maturity is ongoing, but each step forward compounds benefits across the entire software lifecycle.

In the next section, we'll explore why Azure DevOps is particularly well-suited for implementing CI/CD pipelines and how its integrated suite of tools simplifies the journey from code to cloud.

Why Choose Azure DevOps?

Azure DevOps has emerged as a powerful and comprehensive platform for implementing DevOps practices, particularly CI/CD. Built by Microsoft and tightly integrated with the Azure cloud ecosystem, Azure DevOps offers a suite of services that cover every stage of the software development lifecycle—from planning to deployment. But what truly sets it apart is its versatility, extensibility, and robust support for both small teams and enterprise-scale operations.

This section will provide a deep dive into the reasons why organizations across industries choose Azure DevOps for their development and delivery needs, its key advantages, core features, integration capabilities, and how it aligns with modern DevOps goals.

A Unified Platform for the Entire DevOps Lifecycle

Azure DevOps is not a single tool; it's a comprehensive suite designed to support end-to-end DevOps workflows. Instead of stitching together disparate tools for version control, CI/CD, testing, artifact management, and project tracking, Azure DevOps brings everything under one roof.

Core Services Include:

- **Azure Repos** – Git repositories for source control.

- **Azure Pipelines** – CI/CD pipelines with support for both YAML and Classic UI.

- **Azure Boards** – Agile planning, sprint tracking, and issue management.

- **Azure Test Plans** – Manual and automated testing management.

- **Azure Artifacts** – Hosting for NuGet, npm, Maven, and Python packages.

The result is a seamless developer experience where teams can plan, code, build, test, release, and monitor from a single platform.

Cloud-Native and On-Premises Flexibility

Azure DevOps Services (cloud-hosted) and Azure DevOps Server (on-premises) provide deployment flexibility. Organizations that need to meet regulatory or data residency requirements can host Azure DevOps Server on their own infrastructure, while others can benefit from the scalability and maintenance-free nature of the cloud service.

Azure DevOps can also be hybrid—integrating cloud-based pipelines with on-premises build agents or source repositories—giving teams ultimate control over their workflow setup.

First-Class Git Support with Azure Repos

Azure Repos provides distributed version control with Git and centralized control with Team Foundation Version Control (TFVC). Git support is on par with leading Git providers like GitHub, including branch policies, pull requests, and protected branches.

Branch policy example:

1. Require a minimum number of reviewers before merging.

2. Enforce linked work items.

3. Require successful builds before pull request completion.

These policies ensure that only validated and reviewed code makes it into the mainline, improving overall code quality.

Rich YAML Pipeline Support

Azure Pipelines supports both classic UI-based pipelines and **YAML-based** pipelines as code. YAML pipelines provide versionable, declarative control of your CI/CD process, enabling collaboration, reuse, and auditability.

Example YAML Pipeline:

```
trigger:
  branches:
    include:
      - main
```

```
jobs:
- job: Build
  pool:
    vmImage: 'ubuntu-latest'
  steps:
    - task: DotNetCoreCLI@2
      inputs:
        command: 'build'
        projects: '**/*.csproj'
    - task: DotNetCoreCLI@2
      inputs:
        command: 'test'
        projects: '**/*.Tests.csproj'
```

This pipeline builds and tests a .NET Core application, using Microsoft-hosted agents with minimal configuration.

Multi-Platform Support

Azure DevOps supports Windows, Linux, and macOS agents. Whether you're building .NET apps, Node.js APIs, Java services, or iOS applications, Azure DevOps provides the tools to automate your workflows across platforms.

You can install **self-hosted agents** for scenarios that require custom tools or private networking, and **Microsoft-hosted agents** offer convenience and scalability.

Seamless Integration with Azure and Beyond

While Azure DevOps is designed to work natively with Azure cloud services, its integration capabilities are not limited to the Microsoft ecosystem.

Azure-native integrations include:

- Azure App Services for web app deployments

- Azure Kubernetes Service (AKS) for containerized workloads

- Azure Key Vault for secure secret management

- Azure Monitor and Application Insights for observability

External integrations include:

- GitHub, Bitbucket, GitLab for source control

- Jenkins and TeamCity for external CI/CD integration

- Docker Hub and JFrog Artifactory for containers and packages

- Slack, Teams, and email for notifications

Azure DevOps can easily slot into your existing toolchain, ensuring a smooth transition or augmentation of current practices.

Enterprise-Grade Security and Compliance

Security is a first-class concern in Azure DevOps. Features like **fine-grained access control**, **secure pipeline secrets**, and **auditing logs** provide confidence that your processes and data are protected.

Key Security Features:

- Role-Based Access Control (RBAC) for projects, repositories, pipelines, and environments.

- Azure Key Vault integration to store and retrieve secrets during builds and deployments.

- Audit logs to track who did what and when.

- Compliance with standards like ISO 27001, SOC 2, and GDPR.

By incorporating security into every stage of the delivery pipeline (often referred to as **DevSecOps**), Azure DevOps supports modern compliance and governance practices.

Built-in Agile Tools with Azure Boards

Azure Boards provides rich capabilities for managing software projects using Scrum, Kanban, or customized workflows. You can track epics, features, user stories, bugs, and tasks, with full traceability from requirements to release.

Features include:

- Sprint planning and velocity tracking

- Customizable work item types and workflows

- Backlogs and Kanban boards

- Integration with Git commits and pull requests

All work items are linkable to code changes and builds, helping teams maintain traceability and transparency throughout the lifecycle.

Extensibility and Marketplace

Azure DevOps is highly extensible via its REST APIs and a vibrant marketplace. Thousands of extensions are available to enhance functionality, including testing tools, dashboards, notification connectors, and integrations with third-party services.

Popular Marketplace Extensions:

- SonarQube (static code analysis)
- WhiteSource Bolt (license compliance)
- Jira (issue tracking)
- GitHub Actions for Azure Pipelines
- Terraform Tasks

You can also create custom extensions tailored to your organization's needs using the Azure DevOps Extension SDK.

DevOps at Scale

Azure DevOps is designed to support teams of all sizes. Enterprises benefit from features like:

- **Service connections** for managing deployments across environments
- **Environment approvals and gates** for governance
- **Variable groups and templates** for reusability
- **Parallel jobs and deployment slots** for scalability
- **Pipeline caching** to improve build performance

With proper configuration, Azure DevOps can support multiple teams, business units, and environments while maintaining centralized control and visibility.

Global Availability and Reliability

Azure DevOps Services is hosted across multiple geographic regions and offers high availability and disaster recovery features. Microsoft's SLAs and enterprise-grade support ensure that mission-critical CI/CD workflows can run reliably around the clock.

Cost Efficiency and Licensing

Azure DevOps offers a generous free tier for small teams (up to 5 users and unlimited private repos). Paid plans scale based on additional users, build time, and parallel jobs.

You only pay for what you use:

- Additional Microsoft-hosted build minutes beyond free limits
- Additional self-hosted pipelines at scale
- Paid users beyond the free allowance

This pricing flexibility makes Azure DevOps attractive to startups, small businesses, and large enterprises alike.

Real-World Adoption and Ecosystem

Azure DevOps is widely adopted by organizations ranging from government and healthcare to fintech and e-commerce. Its success is fueled by an active user community, extensive documentation, and frequent feature updates.

Case studies from companies like Daimler, HSBC, and L'Oréal showcase how Azure DevOps has enabled global teams to modernize their delivery processes, embrace automation, and scale DevOps practices enterprise-wide.

Summary

Azure DevOps is much more than a CI/CD tool—it's a complete platform for modern DevOps and agile development. By offering integrated tools for planning, building, testing, releasing, and monitoring, Azure DevOps helps teams of all sizes and industries deliver software faster, safer, and more efficiently.

Its cloud-native capabilities, cross-platform support, deep integrations, enterprise readiness, and vibrant ecosystem make it one of the most compelling choices for organizations pursuing DevOps maturity.

In the next section, we'll walk through the structure of this book, highlighting how each chapter builds your understanding of Azure DevOps and equips you with practical knowledge to implement CI/CD pipelines from start to finish.

Overview of the Book Structure

This book is structured to guide you through the complete journey of learning, implementing, and optimizing CI/CD with Azure DevOps. Whether you're entirely new to DevOps or looking to enhance your understanding and deployment practices, the content has been laid out to ensure you build knowledge incrementally—starting with the fundamentals and advancing into real-world implementation scenarios.

The chapters are interconnected and follow a logical progression that mirrors how most software development teams mature their DevOps practices. This section offers a detailed walkthrough of the book's structure, its pedagogical goals, and what you can expect to learn and achieve in each chapter.

Chapter 1: Introduction to CI/CD and Azure DevOps

This opening chapter lays the groundwork by explaining the evolution of software delivery and the emergence of DevOps as a dominant cultural and technical movement. It introduces you to CI/CD principles, the value they bring to modern software development, and why Azure DevOps is one of the best platforms to support them.

You've already seen in this chapter how DevOps has transformed delivery pipelines and how Azure DevOps provides an integrated environment for planning, development, testing, and deployment. This chapter sets the tone for the rest of the book, helping you adopt the right mindset and expectations before diving into the practical elements.

Chapter 2: Setting Up Your Azure DevOps Environment

This chapter walks you through the initial setup required to use Azure DevOps in a real-world context. It includes:

- Creating an Azure DevOps organization.

- Setting up and managing projects.

- Understanding access control and user permissions.

- Configuring connections to external tools like GitHub, Docker Hub, or Jira.

This chapter is especially useful for those in DevOps, DevSecOps, or managerial roles responsible for governance, access management, and foundational infrastructure.

It also includes best practices for organizing multiple projects within a single organization, dealing with billing scopes, and integrating with Azure Active Directory for enterprise-grade identity management.

Chapter 3: Understanding Pipelines in Azure DevOps

Before building your first pipeline, you'll need to understand the anatomy of one. This chapter provides a deep dive into:

- The structure and components of Azure Pipelines.

- Differences between Classic and YAML pipelines.

- Triggers (like push or PR-based builds).

- Pipeline variables, templates, and reusable components.

Expect hands-on examples that illustrate how pipelines are defined, customized, and extended. You'll also learn about pipeline architecture, how builds are queued and executed, and how Azure DevOps uses agents and pools.

By the end of this chapter, you'll be confident in reading and writing YAML pipelines and deciding when to use Classic vs YAML based on your team's needs.

Chapter 4: Building Your First CI Pipeline

This chapter moves from theory to practice by helping you create your first Continuous Integration pipeline. You'll connect your repository (Azure Repos or GitHub), define pipeline tasks, and run your first builds.

Topics include:

- Repository selection and service connections.

- Authoring and validating YAML files.

- Common tasks such as compiling code, restoring packages, and running tests.

- Using pre-defined pipeline tasks and custom scripts.

You'll also explore build validation and status badges—important for maintaining high-quality code in collaborative projects.

Example:

```
trigger:
  branches:
    include:
      - main

steps:
- task: NodeTool@0
  inputs:
    versionSpec: '16.x'
```

```
- script: npm install
- script: npm run build
- script: npm test
```

This code demonstrates a basic Node.js CI pipeline. You'll be able to adapt this structure to other ecosystems such as .NET, Java, or Python.

Chapter 5: Advanced CI Techniques

Once the basics are in place, this chapter guides you into more complex and powerful CI scenarios:

- Multi-stage builds

- Conditional tasks based on environments or variable values

- Generating and managing artifacts

- Integrating code quality gates such as SonarQube or ESLint

- Running parallel jobs and caching dependencies to speed up pipelines

You'll also learn about handling build matrices for different OS/platform combinations—especially useful in open-source or multi-platform development.

By mastering these techniques, your pipelines will be faster, more efficient, and scalable to enterprise-level projects.

Chapter 6: Designing and Deploying CD Pipelines

Transitioning from CI to CD, this chapter focuses on Continuous Delivery and Deployment pipelines. Topics covered include:

- Deployment strategies (manual, semi-automated, automated)

- Environment configuration (development, staging, production)

- Service connections and deployment groups

- Deploying to Azure App Services, Kubernetes, and Virtual Machines

You'll also implement rollback strategies, test in deployment pipelines, and learn how to use approval gates and pre-deployment conditions.

Here, you'll gain fluency in constructing full end-to-end pipelines, making your code ready for production at any moment.

Chapter 7: Security, Compliance, and Best Practices

Security and compliance are critical in any CI/CD workflow. This chapter outlines strategies to secure your pipelines and enforce policies without slowing down delivery.

Covered topics:

- Using secure variables and Azure Key Vault
- Implementing RBAC and fine-grained permissions
- Setting pipeline policies and branch protection rules
- Auditing and logging changes
- Meeting compliance standards like SOC2, HIPAA, or ISO 27001

You'll also learn how to apply the **shift-left security** model by integrating security tests earlier in the pipeline lifecycle.

Chapter 8: Monitoring and Troubleshooting CI/CD Pipelines

No CI/CD system is perfect. Things fail, and this chapter teaches you how to monitor, diagnose, and recover from pipeline issues effectively.

Topics include:

- Logging and telemetry
- Pipeline diagnostics and error tracking
- Real-time alerts and incident management
- Azure Monitor, Log Analytics, and Application Insights
- Root cause analysis and postmortem best practices

You'll also explore patterns for continuous improvement, using feedback from builds and deployments to reduce future errors and improve team velocity.

Chapter 9: Real-World Use Cases and Case Studies

Theory and practice meet in this chapter, where you'll explore real implementations of Azure DevOps pipelines across various industries and scenarios.

Examples include:

- CI/CD for microservices architectures

- Deploying legacy applications using modern pipelines

- Managing multi-tenant deployments and customer-specific branches

- Case studies from major enterprises and startups

Each case study provides pipeline breakdowns, decisions made, challenges encountered, and lessons learned.

This chapter bridges the gap between textbook DevOps and the dynamic realities of production environments.

Chapter 10: Future Trends and Emerging Tools

The DevOps landscape evolves rapidly. This forward-looking chapter covers upcoming trends, tools, and practices that are shaping the next decade of CI/CD.

Topics include:

- GitHub Actions and how it complements Azure DevOps

- The rise of AI in CI/CD (e.g., automatic test generation, anomaly detection)

- Serverless pipelines and ephemeral environments

- CI/CD for machine learning models (MLOps)

- The convergence of DevOps and platform engineering

Understanding these trends will help you future-proof your skills and toolchains, allowing you to adopt or adapt early.

Chapter 11: Appendices

The final section of the book contains practical resources for further learning, hands-on practice, and real-world application:

- **Glossary**: Clear definitions of common DevOps terms.

- **Learning Resources**: Books, videos, certifications, and community forums.

- **Sample Projects**: Mini-projects you can clone, run, and extend.

- **API Reference Guide**: Azure DevOps REST API tips for automation and custom integration.

- **FAQs**: Solutions to common problems and misconceptions.

How to Use This Book

You are encouraged to follow the chapters in order, especially if you are new to Azure DevOps. Each chapter builds on concepts introduced previously. However, experienced readers may choose to jump directly into the sections that are most relevant to their current role or project phase.

The book is designed to be **practical-first**—you'll find code snippets, YAML files, UI walkthroughs, and checklists that you can immediately apply. Key takeaways and summaries at the end of each chapter reinforce what you've learned.

Each chapter also includes "Pro Tips" and "Gotchas" from real-world scenarios, offering actionable insights that go beyond documentation.

Summary

The structure of this book reflects the lifecycle of a DevOps project, beginning with foundational knowledge and culminating in complex, scalable, and secure pipeline solutions. Each chapter is a step forward in your journey toward mastering CI/CD using Azure DevOps.

By the end of this book, you'll not only understand how to create and manage pipelines—you'll also understand how to align DevOps practices with business goals, foster team collaboration, and prepare for the technologies and challenges of tomorrow.

Chapter 2: Setting Up Your Azure DevOps Environment

Creating an Azure DevOps Organization

Before diving into building CI/CD pipelines and managing projects, the first step in your Azure DevOps journey is to set up your Azure DevOps organization. This organization acts as the foundational container where all your DevOps-related activities take place. It encapsulates your projects, users, permissions, repositories, pipelines, boards, artifacts, and more.

In this section, we'll walk through the process of creating an Azure DevOps organization from scratch, configuring initial settings, linking it with Azure Active Directory (if needed), and understanding the implications of region selection, naming conventions, and early governance practices.

What Is an Azure DevOps Organization?

An Azure DevOps organization is a logical boundary for all your development and operations work. It can house multiple projects and helps separate concerns across different teams or departments. You can think of it as the "root" of your DevOps environment, offering control over:

- User   and   group   access

- Policies   and   permissions

- Billing   and   licensing

- Integration   with   identity   providers

- Data   storage   and   location   settings

Each organization is uniquely named and has a region-specific backend to ensure data residency compliance.

Step-by-Step Guide: Creating an Azure DevOps Organization

To create your Azure DevOps organization, follow these steps:

1. **Visit the Azure DevOps Portal:** Go to https://dev.azure.com/ and sign in using your Microsoft account or a work/school account associated with Azure Active Directory.

2. **Create a New Organization:** Once signed in, click the **New organization** button.

Set the Organization Name: Choose a unique name for your organization. This name will be used in your URL:

```
https://dev.azure.com/<organization-name>
```

3. Guidelines:

   - Keep it simple and descriptive.

   - Avoid special characters.

   - It must be globally unique across Azure DevOps.

4. **Choose the Region:** Select a region where your data will be stored. Azure DevOps hosts your data in region-specific data centers. Once selected, the region cannot be changed, so choose wisely, especially if you need to comply with data residency laws.

5. **Create Your First Project:** After creating the organization, you'll be prompted to create a project (you can create more later). Choose:

   - **Project Name**

   - **Visibility**: Public or Private

   - **Version Control**: Git (default) or Team Foundation Version Control (TFVC)

   - **Work Item Process**: Agile, Scrum, CMMI, or Basic

6. You can change the process template later by cloning and customizing it, but it's best to pick the one closest to your methodology upfront.

7. **Confirm and Create:** Click **Create Project**, and your environment will be ready in moments.

Accessing Your Organization Settings

Once your organization is set up, you can access the settings by clicking on the gear icon in the top-right of the Azure DevOps portal. From here, you can manage:

- **Users and Groups**: Add, remove, and manage user roles.

- **Billing**: Choose your pricing tier and manage paid services.

- **Policies**: Set up security controls and permission levels.

- **Auditing and Logs**: View recent activities and changes.

Managing Users and Access Early

Effective DevOps begins with good access control. Azure DevOps supports two identity models:

- **Microsoft Accounts** for individuals and personal use.

- **Azure Active Directory (AAD)** for enterprises and centralized identity management.

If you are using Azure AD:

- Connect your DevOps organization to your AAD tenant.

- Use security groups to control access to projects, repositories, and pipelines.

- Assign roles like **Project Contributor**, **Reader**, **Administrator**, and **Build Administrator**.

To add users:

1. Go to **Organization Settings** > **Users**

2. Click **Add users**

3. Enter email addresses and assign appropriate access level:

   o **Basic**: Standard access for most users (code, pipelines, boards)

   o **Stakeholder**: Lightweight access for managers and stakeholders (view-only boards)

   o **Visual Studio Subscriber**: If you have an MSDN subscription

Managing access early ensures you avoid over-permissioned roles and promotes principle of least privilege.

Billing Considerations

Azure DevOps offers generous free tiers:

- Up to **5** **free** **Basic** **users** per organization

- Unlimited private Git repositories

- 1,800 free build minutes/month for Microsoft-hosted agents

- Unlimited minutes for self-hosted agents

For additional users or parallel jobs, you can scale your billing accordingly via the **Billing** section.

To set up billing:

1. Go to **Organization Settings** > **Billing**

2. Link to your Azure subscription (if not already)

3. Choose between **Basic**, **Basic + Test Plans**, and **Visual Studio subscriber** licenses

Billing is usage-based, and changes can be managed monthly.

Naming Conventions and Project Structure

As your organization grows, establish conventions early for consistency and clarity. Consider these practices:

- Use meaningful organization and project names that reflect business units, teams, or products.

- Standardize repository names, e.g., `web-api`, `mobile-app`, `infra-pipeline`

- Prefix or suffix environment-specific projects, e.g., `myproject-dev`, `myproject-prod`

- Use tags and descriptions to clarify project scope

Example structure:

```
Organization: acme-devops
├── Project: ecommerce-platform
│   ├── Repo: checkout-service
│   ├── Repo: cart-service
│   ├── Pipeline: deploy-checkout
└── Project: internal-tools
    ├── Repo: admin-dashboard
    ├── Pipeline: build-dashboard
```

Configuring Global Settings

Azure DevOps offers several organization-wide configurations that are often overlooked but crucial:

- **Auditing Logs**: Enable to track key events such as permission changes, deletions, and access patterns.

- **Usage Trends**: Understand build usage, repo activity, and work item trends.

- **Policies and Compliance**: Set required reviewers, enforce branch policies, and restrict pipeline execution to trusted sources.

- **Extensions**: Add functionality from the Marketplace for integrations like Jira, SonarQube, Slack, and more.

```
// Sample Azure DevOps API call to list organization projects
GET        https://dev.azure.com/{organization}/_apis/projects?api-
version=7.0
```

Using the Azure DevOps REST API, you can automate environment setup, provisioning of projects, and user management.

Best Practices for Initial Setup

1. **Use Service Connections**: Preconfigure service connections to Azure, GitHub, Docker Hub, etc., to ensure pipelines can authenticate securely.

2. **Define Environments**: Use Azure DevOps Environments feature for development, staging, and production contexts.

3. **Set Up Naming Standards Early**: Maintain clarity and searchability.

4. **Keep Permissions Tight**: Start with minimal access and expand as needed.

5. **Enable Notifications and Alerts**: Get notified about pipeline failures or permission changes.

6. **Enable Retention Policies**: Clean up old pipelines and artifacts to manage storage costs.

Summary

Creating your Azure DevOps organization is the first major milestone in your CI/CD journey. It's more than a signup process—it's where you establish structure, security, and collaboration standards that will impact all future development workflows.

By understanding what an organization is, how to set it up effectively, and what best practices to follow from day one, you're laying a strong foundation for success. From governance and permissions to project and naming conventions, every choice you make here helps define how your team operates in the DevOps lifecycle.

In the next section, we'll dive into how to manage your projects and repositories within this organization, organize your code, and prepare for efficient pipeline integration.

Managing Projects and Repositories

Once your Azure DevOps organization is established, the next critical step is to structure your development work using projects and repositories. Projects in Azure DevOps serve as containers for your code, work items, pipelines, and artifacts. Repositories are where your source code lives and evolves over time. Understanding how to manage these elements effectively is essential for maintaining scalable, secure, and productive DevOps workflows.

This section explores how to create, structure, and maintain projects and repositories within Azure DevOps, covering naming conventions, permissions, branch strategies, repository policies, and lifecycle management.

What Is a Project in Azure DevOps?

A project in Azure DevOps is a logical grouping of all development-related components needed for a software solution. It typically includes:

- **Source** **code** **repositories**
- **Pipelines** **for** **CI/CD**
- **Work** **items** **and** **backlogs**
- **Test** **plans**
- **Artifacts** **(package** **management)**

You can think of a project as a dedicated environment for a team, product, or service. Each project operates independently and can have its own configurations, security, and settings.

While it's technically possible to manage all your work in a single project, separating concerns by domain, team, or product is a best practice for scalability and clarity.

Creating a New Project

To create a new project within your organization:

1. **Navigate   to   Your   Organization**
    Visit `https://dev.azure.com/<your-organization>` and click **New Project**.

2. **Enter   Project   Details**

    o **Project Name**: Clear and descriptive, such as `CustomerPortal`, `MobileApp`,   or   `DevOps-Infrastructure`.

    o **Description**: Optional, but helps clarify purpose for other users.

    o **Visibility**: Choose **Private** (default) to restrict access or **Public** for open-source collaboration.

3. **Advanced   Settings**

    o **Version   Control**:   Git   (recommended)   or   TFVC.

    o **Work Item Process**: Choose from Agile, Scrum, CMMI, or Basic.

4. **Click   Create**
    The   project   will   be   provisioned   and   ready   within   seconds.

You can create multiple projects for separate teams or domains. Avoid cramming unrelated work into a single project as it can lead to confusion and difficulty with permission management.

Repository Management

Repositories (repos) are the backbone of your source code management (SCM). Azure Repos supports **Git**, the most widely used SCM tool, and optionally **TFVC** for legacy use cases.

Each project can host multiple Git repositories. This is helpful when managing microservices, infrastructure code, or modular components within a single team scope.

To create a new repository:

1. Navigate   to   **Repos**   in   your   Azure   DevOps   project.

2. Click   the   drop-down   next   to   the   current   repo   name.

3. Select   **New**   **repository**.

4. Enter   a   **name**,   choose   **Git**,   and   click   **Create**.

You now have a fresh repository ready for your code.

You can also import existing repositories using the **Import** option by supplying a clone URL (HTTP or SSH). This is useful when migrating from GitHub, GitLab, Bitbucket, or other services.

Repository Structure Best Practices

1. Use Clear Naming Conventions

Good names help developers navigate and onboard quickly.

Examples:

- `web-api,` `mobile-client,` `infra-terraform,` `ci-scripts`

Avoid names like `test`, `newrepo`, or `project1` which convey no useful information.

2. Keep Repositories Focused

A single repo should ideally contain only one service or logical component. Avoid monolith repos unless absolutely necessary. If using monorepos, ensure clear folder structures and CI configurations are in place.

Example folder structure:

```
/src
  /api
  /frontend
  /auth-service
/tests
/scripts
```

3. Standardize README and Contributing Files

Every repo should include:

- `README.md` for setup and usage
- `LICENSE` for open-source/legal use
- `.gitignore` to exclude non-essential files
- `CONTRIBUTING.md` to guide collaborators

Branching Strategy

Effective branching strategies are vital for collaboration and release management. Common strategies include:

Git Flow

- **Main**: Production-ready code.

- **Develop**: Active development branch.

- **Feature**: Short-lived branches for new features.

- **Release**: Stabilization before going to production.

- **Hotfix**: Emergency fixes to main.

GitHub Flow (simpler)

- **Main**: Always deployable.

- **Feature branches**: Created from main, merged via PR.

Trunk-Based Development

- All commits go to the main branch with feature toggles.

Choose a model that fits your team size, delivery frequency, and governance requirements.

Implementing Branch Policies

Azure DevOps allows you to enforce branch policies to improve code quality and reduce errors.

To configure policies:

1. Go to **Repos** > **Branches**

2. Click the **three-dot menu** next to your target branch (e.g., main)

3. Select **Branch policies**

Available policy options:

- **Require** a minimum number of reviewers

- **Enforce** successful builds before merging

- **Limit** merge types (e.g., squash only)

- **Check** for linked work items

- **Block** changes with unresolved comments

Example YAML pipeline enforced by branch policy:

```
trigger:
  branches:
    include:
      - main

steps:
  - task: DotNetCoreCLI@2
    inputs:
      command: 'build'
  - task: DotNetCoreCLI@2
    inputs:
      command: 'test'
```

You can even integrate **status checks** from external tools like SonarCloud or WhiteSource.

Repository Permissions and Security

Granular security is essential to protect source code and ensure that developers only have access to what they need.

Permissions can be applied at:

- Project   level

- Repository   level

- Branch   level

Common roles:

- **Contributor**:   Can   read/write   code   and   push   changes

- **Reader**: Can only read
- **Administrator**: Full access including policy configuration

To assign permissions:

1. Navigate to **Project Settings** > **Repositories**
2. Choose a repo, then select **Security**
3. Add users/groups and define access levels

Git Tags and Releases

Azure DevOps supports Git tags to mark release versions. These are especially useful for:

- Creating semantic versioning (v1.0.0, v2.1.3)
- Marking hotfixes and rollback points
- Automating release notes generation

You can create tags via CLI:

```
git tag -a v1.0.0 -m "Initial release"
git push origin v1.0.0
```

Or automate tagging through pipelines using custom scripts and the REST API.

Repository Cleanup and Lifecycle

Over time, repositories accumulate stale branches, unused files, and legacy code. Set up periodic maintenance tasks such as:

- **Deleting merged branches**
- **Archiving deprecated repositories**
- **Reviewing contributor activity**
- **Rotating credentials and access tokens**
- **Running code cleanup tools**

You can enforce branch cleanup via retention policies in pipeline settings or through scheduled scripts.

Integrations and Webhooks

Azure Repos supports webhooks and service connections for seamless integrations. For example:

- Triggering Jenkins or GitHub Actions workflows on commits

- Sending Slack or Teams notifications on PR events

- Posting build statuses to external dashboards

To add a webhook:

1. Go to **Project Settings > Service Hooks**

2. Select the service (e.g., Slack)

3. Define the trigger and payload

For example, notify Slack on pull request creation:

```
{
  "eventType": "pullrequest.created",
  "url": "https://hooks.slack.com/services/your-webhook-url",
  "resourceVersion": "1.0"
}
```

Summary

Managing projects and repositories effectively is one of the foundational responsibilities in Azure DevOps. A well-structured project, supported by secure, scalable repositories and thoughtful branching strategies, sets your team up for long-term success.

From creating projects to organizing source code and enforcing branch policies, Azure DevOps provides a rich feature set for teams of all sizes. By following naming conventions, applying access control, and leveraging automation tools, your repositories can evolve in tandem with your product and delivery goals.

In the next section, we'll explore how to configure permissions and access control across projects, pipelines, and environments—ensuring the right people have the right level of access at all times.

Configuring Permissions and Access Control

Effective permissions and access control are foundational pillars of a secure and maintainable Azure DevOps environment. As organizations scale and multiple teams begin interacting with repositories, pipelines, boards, and artifacts, properly managing access is essential for enforcing the principle of least privilege, maintaining auditability, and preventing accidental or malicious changes.

This section explores in depth how Azure DevOps manages identity and access across organizations, projects, and resources. You'll learn how to configure permissions for individuals and groups, set access levels, establish governance policies, integrate with Azure Active Directory, and automate access management where necessary.

Identity Management in Azure DevOps

Azure DevOps supports two main identity systems:

1. **Microsoft Accounts** (MSA): Ideal for individuals or small teams using personal Microsoft accounts (e.g., Outlook.com, Hotmail).

2. **Azure Active Directory (AAD)**: Recommended for enterprise teams needing centralized user and group management, integration with Microsoft 365, and security governance.

When connected to an Azure AD tenant, Azure DevOps can leverage AAD users and security groups, enabling scalable and maintainable permission structures.

To link an Azure DevOps organization to Azure AD:

- Navigate to **Organization Settings** > **Azure Active Directory**

- Click **Connect directory**

- Select your tenant (you must be a global admin)

This unlocks enterprise features like group-based security assignment, tenant policy enforcement, and seamless user provisioning.

Access Levels vs Permissions

Azure DevOps separates **access levels** from **permissions**, which are often mistakenly conflated.

- **Access Levels** determine which features a user can *see* (e.g., Boards, Pipelines, Test Plans).

- **Permissions** determine what actions a user can *perform* (e.g., edit pipelines, delete repos).

Access Levels:

- **Stakeholder**: Free, limited access to Boards and work items.

- **Basic**: Standard access to most features (Boards, Repos, Pipelines, Artifacts).

- **Basic + Test Plans**: Includes Test Plans feature.

- **Visual Studio Subscriber**: Access based on MSDN license entitlement.

To assign access levels:

1. Go to **Organization Settings > Users**

2. Click on a user's name

3. Select an access level from the dropdown

Permissions are resource-specific and highly granular. They can be configured at the level of:

- Organization

- Project

- Repositories

- Pipelines

- Environments

- Agent pools

- Service connections

Understanding Security Groups

Azure DevOps comes with built-in security groups, including:

- **Project Administrators**

- **Contributors**

- **Readers**

- **Build**   **Administrators**

- **Release**   **Administrators**

You can also create **custom groups** to define roles like DevOps Engineers, QA, Product Managers, etc., and assign permissions according to your organization's RBAC (Role-Based Access Control) model.

To create a custom group:

1. Go   to   **Project   Settings   >   Permissions**

2. Click   **New   Group**

3. Name   the   group   and   add   members

4. Define   specific   permissions   for   each   resource   (Repos,   Pipelines,   Boards)

Repository Permissions

Repository permissions govern who can access and modify source code.

Typical permissions include:

- **Read**:   View   the   repository

- **Contribute**:   Push   and   pull   code

- **Branch   Create/Delete**:   Create   and   manage   branches

- **Force   Push**:   Rewrite   history   (should   be   disabled   unless   necessary)

To manage repo permissions:

1. Go   to   **Project   Settings   >   Repositories**

2. Choose   a   repository

3. Click   **Security**

4. Assign   permissions   to   users   or   groups

Example: Only allow senior engineers to delete branches or perform force pushes. All others get Read/Contribute access only.

```
git branch -D feature/unstable  # restricted for most users
```

Pipeline Permissions

Azure Pipelines also have permission boundaries. You can control:

- Who can view/edit pipelines

- Who can queue builds or releases

- Who can approve deployments to environments

- Who can manage agent pools

For YAML pipelines:

- Permissions apply at the pipeline file's repo level.

- Use **branch protection policies** to restrict who can modify pipeline definitions.

For Classic pipelines:

- Go to **Pipelines > [Your Pipeline] > More Options > Security**

Key Permission Examples:

- **Queue builds:** Allow team leads and automation accounts

- **Edit pipeline:** Restrict to DevOps team

- **View builds:** Grant broadly to encourage transparency

Environment and Deployment Permissions

Azure DevOps Environments are used in CD pipelines to model deployment stages like Development, QA, Staging, and Production. These environments can have **approval gates** and **deployment restrictions**.

To configure environment permissions:

1. Go to **Pipelines** > **Environments**

2. Select an environment

3. Click **More** **Options** > **Security**

Example Use Case:

- Developers can deploy to QA

- Only QA team can deploy to Staging

- Only Ops team can approve Production releases

You can also enforce **manual approval gates** using environment permissions or **pipeline approvals** in multi-stage YAML pipelines:

```
environments:
- environment: 'Production'
  approval:
    approvals:
      - reviewers:
          - id: '<user-id>'
            type: User
```

Service Connections

Service connections allow pipelines to authenticate to Azure, Docker Hub, GitHub, AWS, and other external systems.

These connections should be secured tightly, as they often carry significant privileges.

Best practices:

- Use **managed** **identities** for Azure resources

- Limit access to service connections by restricting pipeline usage

- Set connection-specific permissions under **Project Settings > Service Connections**

You can restrict which users/pipelines can use a service connection:

- Go to the connection → **Security**

- Set **"Use"**, **"Manage"**, or **"Administer"** rights per group/user

Agent Pools and Permissions

Build and deployment agents run your CI/CD jobs. Azure DevOps allows control over who can access and manage agent pools.

Typical scenarios:

- Dev team can use `default` pool for CI jobs

- Ops team can use `self-hosted-linux` for production deployments

- Only administrators can delete or modify pools

To assign agent pool permissions:

1. Go to **Organization Settings > Agent Pools**

2. Choose a pool

3. Select **Security**

Permissions include:

- **Use Pool**

- **Manage Pool**

- **Administer**

Restrict high-privilege pools to reduce security exposure.

Audit and Compliance

All access and permission changes are recorded in the **Audit Logs**, available from **Organization Settings > Auditing**.

Auditable events include:

- Adding/removing users

- Granting/revoking permissions

- Changes to pipelines, repos, and service connections

Export these logs to SIEM tools (e.g., Microsoft Sentinel, Splunk) for advanced monitoring and compliance tracking.

Automation and Scripting

Permissions can be managed programmatically using the **Azure DevOps REST API** or CLI tools such as `az devops`.

Example: Add user to a project group via CLI

```
az devops security group membership add \
  --group-id <group-id> \
  --member-id <user-id> \
  --org https://dev.azure.com/<organization> \
  --project <project-name>
```

This is particularly useful when onboarding large teams or rotating secrets/roles on schedule.

You can also automate periodic permission reviews or cleanup tasks with scheduled PowerShell or Python scripts.

Best Practices Summary

- **Use Azure AD integration** for centralized identity and group management.

- **Favor groups over individual permissions** for easier auditing and scalability.

- **Assign minimum necessary permissions** to enforce least privilege.

- **Audit high-risk actions** like service connection usage, production deployments, and pipeline edits.

- **Segment environments and repos** so teams only access what's relevant.

- **Review access regularly**, especially when employees change roles or leave.

Summary

Managing permissions and access control in Azure DevOps is more than a checkbox exercise—it's a critical part of creating a secure, scalable, and collaborative development environment. Whether you're running a small team or a global DevOps operation, understanding how access levels, roles, and permissions interact gives you the power to control risk, improve accountability, and streamline development workflows.

In the next section, we'll explore how to integrate Azure DevOps with external tools and services to enhance automation, testing, collaboration, and security in your CI/CD pipelines.

Integrating External Tools and Services

While Azure DevOps offers a comprehensive suite of features—covering source control, CI/CD pipelines, work item tracking, and more—its true power lies in its ability to integrate seamlessly with a wide array of external tools and services. These integrations enhance productivity, enable richer DevOps workflows, improve quality assurance, and support collaboration across different platforms and disciplines.

This section provides a deep and practical exploration of how to connect Azure DevOps with external systems such as GitHub, Slack, Jira, Docker Hub, Kubernetes, SonarQube, Terraform, Microsoft Teams, and more. You'll learn how to set up service connections, configure webhooks, use extensions, automate cross-platform tasks, and leverage Azure DevOps as a central hub in a connected development ecosystem.

Categories of Integrations

External integrations typically fall into the following categories:

- **Source Control Integrations** (e.g., GitHub, Bitbucket)

- **Notification and Chat Ops** (e.g., Slack, Teams)

- **Issue and Project Tracking** (e.g., Jira, ServiceNow)

- **Container Registries and Orchestration** (e.g., Docker Hub, Kubernetes)

- **Security and Quality Tools** (e.g., SonarQube, WhiteSource, Checkmarx)

- **Infrastructure as Code** (e.g., Terraform, Pulumi)

- **Monitoring and Observability** (e.g., Azure Monitor, Datadog)

- **Testing and QA** (e.g., Postman, Selenium Grid, BrowserStack)

Azure DevOps enables these integrations using **Service Connections**, **Webhooks**, **Marketplace Extensions**, and **REST APIs**.

GitHub Integration

Despite Azure DevOps including its own Git service (Azure Repos), many teams use GitHub for source control. Azure DevOps supports first-class integration with GitHub repositories, enabling you to trigger builds, run pull request validations, and deploy code from GitHub-hosted repos.

To connect a GitHub repo to Azure DevOps Pipelines:

1. Navigate to **Pipelines > New Pipeline**

2. Choose **GitHub** as the source

3. Authenticate using OAuth or a GitHub token

4. Select the repo and define a YAML pipeline

Sample YAML triggered by GitHub:

```
trigger:
  branches:
    include:
      - main

pool:
  vmImage: 'ubuntu-latest'

steps:
  - task: NodeTool@0
    inputs:
      versionSpec: '16.x'
  - script: npm install
  - script: npm run build
```

For pull request validations:

- Set branch policies on your Azure DevOps pipeline
- Use GitHub Checks API to report build status

Slack and Microsoft Teams

Real-time notifications play a vital role in DevOps. Azure DevOps can push updates to **Slack** or **Microsoft Teams** to inform teams about build completions, PRs, code pushes, and deployment status.

To connect Azure DevOps to Slack:

1. Go to **Project Settings > Service Hooks**
2. Choose **Slack**
3. Select the event (e.g., build succeeded, PR created)
4. Paste your Slack webhook URL
5. Customize the payload as needed

Example payload for a PR creation:

```
{
  "text": "A new Pull Request has been created by @john.doe: [Fix login issue](https://dev.azure.com/org/project/_git/repo/pullrequest/1)"
}
```

For **Teams**, install the Azure DevOps connector from the Teams app store, then configure which events to send to the channel.

Benefits:

- Real-time visibility
- Immediate feedback on issues
- Encourages rapid collaboration and resolution

Jira and Work Item Synchronization

Azure Boards provides powerful work item tracking, but some organizations prefer to use **Jira** for project management. Azure DevOps supports bidirectional synchronization of work items and development activity between Jira and Azure DevOps.

Via Marketplace Extension:

- Install the **Jira Integration** extension
- Authenticate using API tokens

- Map Azure DevOps work items to Jira issues

Via REST API/Webhooks:

- Use Azure DevOps webhooks to trigger updates to Jira via custom middleware

- Use Jira webhooks to sync back to Azure

Use case example:

- Developer pushes code to Azure DevOps repo

- Commits contain Jira ticket ID (ABC-123)

- Build pipeline includes a step to update ticket status or comment

---

Docker Hub and Container Registries

CI/CD pipelines in Azure DevOps often include containerization workflows. You can push and pull images from:

- Docker Hub

- Azure Container Registry (ACR)

- Amazon ECR

- GitHub Container Registry

To integrate Docker Hub:

1. Go to **Project Settings > Service Connections**
2. Select **Docker Registry**
3. Enter Docker Hub credentials or token
4. Use this connection in a pipeline

Sample YAML:

```
steps:
```

```
- task: Docker@2
  inputs:
    command: 'buildAndPush'
    containerRegistry: 'dockerhub-connection'
    repository: 'myorg/myapp'
    Dockerfile: '**/Dockerfile'
    tags: '$(Build.BuildId)'
```

Security Tip: Use **secrets** or **Azure Key Vault** for storing Docker credentials securely.

Kubernetes and Helm Deployments

Azure DevOps supports Kubernetes-based deployments using:

- Azure Kubernetes Service (AKS)

- Self-managed clusters

- Helm charts

To set up Kubernetes integration:

1. Create a **Kubernetes service connection**

2. Configure pipeline tasks to apply manifests or deploy Helm charts

Example pipeline task:

```
- task: Kubernetes@1
  inputs:
    connectionType: 'Kubernetes Service Connection'
    kubernetesServiceEndpoint: 'aks-connection'
    command: 'apply'
    useConfigurationFile: true
    configuration: 'manifests/deployment.yaml'
```

Advanced features:

- Blue/green deployments

- Canary   releases

- Secrets   management   with   Azure   Key   Vault   +   Kubernetes   CSI   driver

---

SonarQube and Code Quality Gates

Static analysis is crucial for preventing bugs and enforcing code standards. Azure DevOps integrates well with **SonarQube** for automated code analysis.

Steps:

1. Install   **SonarQube   Extension**   from   the   Marketplace

2. Set   up   a   SonarQube   server   or   use   **SonarCloud**

3. Add   tasks   to   your   pipeline:

```
- task: SonarQubePrepare@5
  inputs:
    SonarQube: 'sonarqube-connection'
    scannerMode: 'CLI'
    configMode: 'manual'
    cliProjectKey: 'project-key'
    cliProjectName: 'My App'

- script: dotnet build

- task: SonarQubeAnalyze@5

- task: SonarQubePublish@5
  inputs:
    pollingTimeoutSec: '300'
```

Quality gates can block pull requests or deployments if code coverage or vulnerability thresholds are not met.

Infrastructure as Code Tools (Terraform, Pulumi)

Azure DevOps Pipelines can execute Terraform or Pulumi scripts to provision and manage cloud infrastructure.

Example Terraform Task:

```
- task: TerraformInstaller@0
  inputs:
    terraformVersion: '1.3.0'

- task: TerraformTaskV4@4
  inputs:
    provider: 'azurerm'
    command: 'apply'
    workingDirectory: 'infra'
    environmentServiceNameAzureRM: 'azure-connection'
```

Best Practices:

- Store state in remote backends (e.g., Azure Storage)
- Use service principals with least privilege
- Include validation and formatting steps

Testing Tools (Postman, Selenium, BrowserStack)

For testing integrations:

- Use **Newman CLI** to run Postman collections
- Integrate **Selenium Grid** tests as build steps
- Use **BrowserStack** for cross-browser UI tests

Sample Postman test:

```
- script: |
    npm install -g newman
    newman run tests/collection.json --environment tests/env.json
  displayName: 'Run API Tests'
```

Marketplace Extensions

Azure DevOps has a rich **Marketplace** offering hundreds of extensions for analytics, monitoring, testing, integration, DevSecOps, and more.

Popular extensions:

- **WhiteSource** **Bolt**: License compliance
- **Terraform**: IaC automation
- **Jira** **Connector**
- **GitHub** **Checks**
- **AWS** **Toolkit**
- **Artifactory** **Integration**

To install:

1. Go to **Organization** **Settings** **>** **Extensions**
2. Browse and install from the Marketplace
3. Enable for the relevant projects

Using REST APIs for Custom Integrations

You can build highly customized integrations using the Azure DevOps REST APIs.

Example: List projects via API

```
GET           https://dev.azure.com/{organization}/_apis/projects?api-
version=7.0
Authorization: Basic {PAT}
```

Use cases:

- Custom dashboards
- ChatOps bots
- Automated incident reporting

- Cross-system work item sync

Secure your APIs using **Personal Access Tokens (PAT)** or **OAuth** tokens. Rotate credentials regularly and assign minimal scopes.

Summary

Integrating Azure DevOps with external tools and services significantly expands its capabilities, enabling end-to-end automation, improved collaboration, and deeper visibility across your delivery pipelines. Whether you're linking with GitHub, deploying to Kubernetes, analyzing code with SonarQube, or syncing work with Jira, these integrations create a unified ecosystem that empowers your team to deliver high-quality software at speed.

By strategically leveraging service connections, webhooks, extensions, and APIs, Azure DevOps becomes not just a CI/CD tool—but the central nervous system of your software delivery pipeline.

In the next chapter, we will explore the anatomy of Azure Pipelines, compare YAML and Classic formats, and break down how to architect robust, scalable CI/CD workflows.

Chapter 3: Understanding Pipelines in Azure DevOps

Core Concepts of Build and Release Pipelines

In any modern DevOps workflow, CI/CD pipelines serve as the backbone of automated software delivery. Azure DevOps provides a robust and scalable pipeline framework that allows development teams to continuously integrate code changes and deliver software faster, with higher confidence. This section explores the foundational concepts that define Azure Pipelines, focusing on the fundamental differences between build and release pipelines, their purposes, components, and how they interact throughout the software development lifecycle.

What Are CI/CD Pipelines?

A pipeline in Azure DevOps is a set of automated processes that enable you to build, test, and deploy your code consistently and efficiently. CI (Continuous Integration) refers to the practice of merging all developers' working copies to a shared mainline several times a day. CD (Continuous Delivery or Deployment) extends CI by automating the release of these changes to production or other environments.

The benefits of CI/CD include:

- **Improved code quality** through continuous testing and validation.

- **Faster feedback loops** allowing developers to address issues early.

- **Reduced deployment risks** due to smaller, incremental changes.

- **Increased confidence in releases**, enabling faster go-to-market timelines.

Azure Pipelines supports both **YAML-based pipelines** and **Classic UI-based pipelines**, offering flexibility for different team preferences and levels of expertise.

Build Pipelines vs. Release Pipelines

Azure DevOps originally distinguished between two types of pipelines:

1. **Build Pipelines**: Primarily focused on compiling code, running unit tests, and producing build artifacts. This process verifies that code changes do not break the application and that they integrate cleanly with the existing codebase.

2. **Release Pipelines**: Focused on deploying build artifacts to various environments (e.g., dev, test, staging, production). These pipelines often include approval gates, automated tests, and rollback strategies to ensure safe delivery.

With the introduction of **multi-stage YAML pipelines**, the lines between build and release pipelines have blurred. Now, a single YAML pipeline can handle both CI and CD processes, offering a streamlined and maintainable workflow.

Pipeline Components

An Azure DevOps pipeline consists of several key components:

- **Triggers**: Events that start the pipeline, such as pushing code to a branch or creating a pull request.

- **Stages**: Logical groupings of jobs that represent a phase in the pipeline (e.g., build, test, deploy).

- **Jobs**: A set of steps that run on the same agent. Each job is isolated and may run on different environments.

- **Steps**: Individual tasks or scripts executed during the pipeline. Steps can install dependencies, run tests, or publish artifacts.

- **Artifacts**: The output of a pipeline, such as compiled binaries or container images, which can be deployed in later stages.

- **Environments**: Target destinations for deployments. Environments can be linked with approvals and checks for governance.

Understanding how these pieces fit together is critical for designing effective pipelines.

Multi-Stage Pipelines

A multi-stage pipeline enables you to define both CI and CD in a single YAML file. This approach has numerous advantages:

- **Unified workflow**: Easier to manage and visualize the entire pipeline.

- **Version control**: YAML pipelines are stored alongside your code, enabling changes to be tracked and reviewed.

- **Modularization**: You can break down pipelines into reusable templates and components.

Here's an example of a basic multi-stage pipeline:

```
trigger:
  branches:
    include:
      - main

stages:
- stage: Build
  jobs:
  - job: BuildJob
    pool:
      vmImage: 'ubuntu-latest'
    steps:
    - task: UseNode@2
      inputs:
        version: '16.x'
    - script: npm install
    - script: npm run build
    - task: PublishBuildArtifacts@1
      inputs:
        pathToPublish: 'dist'
        artifactName: 'drop'

- stage: Deploy
  dependsOn: Build
  condition: succeeded()
  jobs:
  - deployment: DeployJob
    environment: 'staging'
    strategy:
      runOnce:
        deploy:
          steps:
            - download: current
              artifact: drop
            - script: echo "Deploying to staging..."
```

This pipeline defines two stages: `Build` and `Deploy`. The build stage installs dependencies, compiles the code, and publishes the artifact. The deploy stage then downloads the artifact and simulates a deployment to a staging environment.

Agents and Pools

Pipelines are executed on agents — machines that run the steps defined in your pipeline. Azure provides two types of agents:

- **Microsoft-hosted agents**: Pre-configured environments provided by Azure. Ideal for most CI/CD scenarios.

- **Self-hosted agents**: Custom machines you manage. Suitable for scenarios requiring specific tools, software, or isolation.

Agent pools group agents to manage workload distribution and scale. Each job in your pipeline is assigned to an agent from a pool.

You can specify an agent like this in YAML:

```
pool:
  vmImage: 'windows-latest'
```

Or for a self-hosted pool:

```
pool:
  name: 'MySelfHostedPool'
```

Variables and Templates

Variables make pipelines more flexible and reusable. You can define variables at the pipeline, stage, or job level.

```
variables:
  buildConfiguration: 'Release'
  nodeVersion: '16.x'
```

Templates allow you to reuse pipeline configurations. For example, you can define a template file called `build-template.yml`:

```
# build-template.yml
```

```
parameters:
  - name: buildConfiguration
    default: 'Release'

steps:
- script: echo "Building with ${{ parameters.buildConfiguration }}"
```

Then use it in your main pipeline:

```
extends:
  template: build-template.yml
  parameters:
    buildConfiguration: 'Debug'
```

This promotes DRY (Don't Repeat Yourself) principles and makes complex pipelines easier to manage.

Triggers and Scheduling

You can trigger pipelines manually, on schedule, or automatically via events:

- **Continuous Integration (CI)**: Triggered on code changes.

- **Scheduled Runs**: Using cron syntax.

- **Pipeline Completion**: One pipeline starts after another completes.

Example of a scheduled trigger:

```
schedules:
- cron: "0 2 * * 1"
  displayName: Weekly Monday Run
  branches:
    include:
      - main
```

This example runs the pipeline every Monday at 2:00 AM UTC on the main branch.

Conclusion

Understanding the core concepts of Azure DevOps pipelines is crucial for building efficient, maintainable, and scalable CI/CD processes. By mastering the elements discussed — such as stages, jobs, triggers, templates, and environments — you lay the foundation for automating your software delivery pipeline. This knowledge sets the stage for hands-on creation and customization of pipelines, which we'll explore in the next chapters as we dive into building real-world CI and CD workflows.

YAML vs Classic Pipelines

Azure DevOps offers two main approaches to defining and managing pipelines: **YAML pipelines** and **Classic (UI-based) pipelines**. While both achieve the same end goal — automating build, test, and deployment processes — the approach, flexibility, and usability differ significantly. Understanding these differences, their strengths and limitations, and when to use each is critical for designing an efficient DevOps workflow tailored to your team and project needs.

What Is a YAML Pipeline?

YAML pipelines are defined using a .yml file checked into the source code repository. This file contains all the pipeline configuration — from triggers to build steps and deployments — written in a human-readable, structured format.

A typical YAML pipeline might look like this:

```
trigger:
  branches:
    include:
      - main

pool:
  vmImage: 'ubuntu-latest'

steps:
- task: NodeTool@0
  inputs:
    versionSpec: '16.x'
- script: npm install
- script: npm run build
```

Key characteristics of YAML pipelines:

- **Code as configuration**: Pipelines are version-controlled, peer-reviewed, and can evolve with the codebase.

- **Reusable and modular**: Supports templates and variables for DRY practices.

- **Multi-stage support**: CI and CD can be unified in a single pipeline definition.

- **Full auditability**: Changes to the pipeline are traceable via git history.

What Is a Classic Pipeline?

Classic pipelines are configured via the Azure DevOps web portal using a graphical user interface. You define your pipeline using a series of dropdowns, inputs, and task selectors.

Classic pipeline characteristics:

- **UI-driven**: No code writing required — good for those less comfortable with YAML.

- **Separation of concerns**: CI and CD are typically managed in separate pipeline definitions (build pipeline vs. release pipeline).

- **Ideal for legacy or simple scenarios**: Particularly when working with teams unfamiliar with infrastructure as code.

Comparison: YAML vs Classic Pipelines

Feature	YAML Pipelines	Classic Pipelines
Definition	Code file (.yml)	UI-based (web portal)
Version Control	Stored in Git repository	Not tracked in Git
Reviewability	Reviewed like any other code	Manual configuration changes
Reusability (Templates)	Strong template and parameter support	Limited or none
Multi-Stage Support	Full CI/CD in one pipeline	Split between Build and Release pipelines

Auditability	Changes are part of source control	Changes tracked in Azure DevOps UI only
Learning Curve	Requires YAML knowledge	Easier for beginners
Best for	Teams using GitOps and automation	Teams preferring UI or quick setups

Benefits of YAML Pipelines

1. Unified Configuration

YAML pipelines consolidate build, test, and deployment into a single file. This eliminates the need for managing separate build and release definitions and makes your pipeline easier to reason about.

```
stages:
- stage: Build
  jobs:
    - job: BuildApp
      steps:
        - script: dotnet build

- stage: Deploy
  jobs:
    - job: DeployApp
      steps:
        - script: az webapp deploy
```

With this structure, you can visualize the entire lifecycle of your code from commit to production within a single file.

2. Templating and Reusability

You can break pipelines into templates, making them easier to maintain. For example, you might define a reusable build step in build-template.yml:

```
# build-template.yml
parameters:
  - name: solution
    type: string
```

```
steps:
- script: dotnet build ${{ parameters.solution }}
```

And then include it in your pipeline:

```
extends:
  template: build-template.yml
  parameters:
    solution: '**/*.sln'
```

This modular approach scales well across multiple repositories and teams.

3. Better Collaboration

Since YAML is stored in Git, teams can:

- Collaborate on pipeline changes using pull requests.

- Review and discuss pipeline updates in code reviews.

- Roll back to previous versions easily.

Benefits of Classic Pipelines

1. Simplicity and Accessibility

Classic pipelines are easier for new users or non-developers. Users can:

- Create pipelines with clicks rather than code.

- Drag and drop steps to change build order.

- Use wizards to connect repositories and add tasks.

2. Mature UI for Release Management

Classic release pipelines offer a robust interface for managing deployments across multiple environments, complete with:

- Approval gates (pre- and post-deployment).

- Manual intervention tasks.

- Environment-specific   variables.

This makes them ideal for complex enterprise release workflows where manual control and visibility are essential.

Drawbacks of Each Approach

YAML Pipeline Limitations

- **Learning curve**: YAML syntax can be verbose and error-prone, especially for newcomers.

- **Debugging**: Debugging YAML errors can be tricky due to limited error context.

- **Initial setup**: Requires familiarity with DevOps concepts to structure properly.

Classic Pipeline Limitations

- **No version control**: You can't track changes in Git, leading to audit challenges.

- **Harder to replicate**: Duplicating a pipeline across projects or teams requires manual effort.

- **Fragmentation**: Build and release logic often ends up in separate definitions, complicating   the   overall   picture.

Transitioning from Classic to YAML

Many organizations start with Classic pipelines and gradually move to YAML for its long-term maintainability and scalability. Azure DevOps supports this transition through:

- **Export options**: Classic build pipelines can be exported as YAML.

- **Dual usage**: You can run YAML pipelines for CI and use classic releases for CD as an   interim   step.

Steps to transition:

1. Start   by   exporting   a   build   pipeline   to   YAML:

  - Go to the Classic pipeline > Edit > View YAML.

2. Replace the classic release pipeline by building a multi-stage YAML pipeline.

3. Store the YAML in your repository, ideally under `.azure-pipelines/` directory.

When to Use YAML vs Classic

Use YAML when:

- You want pipeline-as-code with version control.

- Your team is familiar with YAML or DevOps tooling.

- You need reusable, templated pipeline components.

- You're working on complex, multi-stage delivery pipelines.

Use Classic when:

- You're quickly prototyping or demoing something.

- You're working with teams unfamiliar with YAML or Git.

- You require a GUI-based release management system with extensive manual approvals.

- Your application lifecycle involves heavy manual QA and sign-offs.

Real-World Considerations

In large enterprises, it's common to find both pipeline types in use. A legacy team may stick with Classic pipelines due to historical reasons or lower technical experience, while new microservice teams adopt YAML-first pipelines for speed and automation.

Organizations that enforce compliance or need audit trails often prefer YAML for its visibility and traceability. Furthermore, when integrated with GitOps workflows, YAML enables fully automated deployments through pull request approvals and infrastructure as code practices.

YAML Best Practices

- **Use templates** for reusable logic (e.g., standard build and test procedures).

- **Store pipeline files with the code** to ensure they evolve together.

- **Use parameters and variables** for environment-specific customization.

- **Keep stages logically separated** (e.g., build, test, deploy).

- **Use** `condition` **statements** to control flow dynamically.

Example of a conditional job:

```
jobs:
- job: RunTests
  condition: and(succeeded(), eq(variables['Build.SourceBranch'],
'refs/heads/main'))
  steps:
    - script: npm test
```

This job only runs if the previous step succeeded *and* the branch is `main`.

Conclusion

Both YAML and Classic pipelines are powerful tools in the Azure DevOps ecosystem, but they cater to different audiences and use cases. YAML pipelines offer the power, portability, and maintainability needed for modern DevOps practices, especially in Git-centric environments. Classic pipelines, on the other hand, serve well in scenarios where simplicity, visual management, and step-by-step guidance are prioritized.

Ultimately, the decision isn't always binary — many teams use a hybrid model and transition over time. What's important is choosing a pipeline strategy that aligns with your team's skills, project needs, and long-term automation goals. As DevOps maturity grows, the industry trend is clearly moving toward YAML as the standard for pipeline-as-code and continuous delivery.

Pipeline Structure and Syntax

Understanding the structure and syntax of Azure DevOps YAML pipelines is essential for constructing reliable and maintainable continuous integration and continuous deployment (CI/CD) workflows. YAML (YAML Ain't Markup Language) offers a clear, structured, and human-readable way to define automation steps, but it also requires precision in indentation and format.

This section breaks down the anatomy of a YAML pipeline in Azure DevOps, discusses each element in detail, and provides practical examples to help you build pipelines confidently. We'll cover everything from pipeline-level properties to deeply nested job configurations, reusable patterns, and more.

Core Structure of a YAML Pipeline

A YAML pipeline in Azure DevOps typically includes the following top-level components:

- `trigger`: Defines when the pipeline runs.

- `pool`: Specifies the agent pool or image used to run the pipeline.

- `variables`: Defines global or scoped variables.

- `stages`: High-level grouping of jobs.

- `jobs`: Collections of steps that run on the same agent.

- `steps`: Actions such as tasks, scripts, or template calls.

Here's a minimal but valid structure:

```yaml
trigger:
  branches:
    include:
      - main

pool:
  vmImage: 'ubuntu-latest'

variables:
  buildConfiguration: 'Release'

stages:
- stage: Build
  jobs:
  - job: BuildApp
    steps:
    - script: dotnet build --configuration $(buildConfiguration)
```

Let's break down each of these elements in more detail.

Trigger

The `trigger` section specifies which branch commits will automatically start the pipeline.

```
trigger:
  branches:
    include:
      - main
      - develop
```

You can also exclude branches:

```
trigger:
  branches:
    exclude:
      - experimental/*
```

And if you want to disable CI triggers entirely:

```
trigger: none
```

For pull request validation:

```
pr:
  branches:
    include:
      - main
```

Pool

Defines the agent the job will run on. Azure DevOps offers Microsoft-hosted agents or your own self-hosted ones.

```
pool:
  vmImage: 'windows-latest'
```

To use a self-hosted pool:

```
pool:
  name: 'MyPrivatePool'
```

Variables

Variables are used to define reusable values. They can be scoped globally, per stage, or per job.

```
variables:
  nodeVersion: '18.x'
  buildConfiguration: 'Release'
```

You can also reference variable groups:

```
variables:
- group: 'SharedSecrets'
```

And use them like this:

```
- script: echo "Building with configuration $(buildConfiguration)"
```

Azure DevOps supports runtime expressions:

```
- script: echo "Branch is $[variables['Build.SourceBranch']]"
```

Stages

Stages allow you to group jobs logically. Each stage can represent a part of the pipeline — such as build, test, or deploy.

```
stages:
- stage: Build
  displayName: 'Build Stage'
  jobs:
    - job: BuildJob
      steps:
        - script: echo Building app
- stage: Deploy
  dependsOn: Build
```

```
condition: succeeded()
jobs:
  - job: DeployJob
    steps:
      - script: echo Deploying app
```

Stages can have conditions, environments, approvals, and checks.

Jobs

Each job runs on a single agent. Jobs can be run sequentially or in parallel.

```
jobs:
- job: TestJob
  pool:
    vmImage: 'ubuntu-latest'
  steps:
    - script: npm test
```

You can also define dependencies between jobs:

```
jobs:
- job: Build
  steps:
    - script: echo Building
- job: Test
  dependsOn: Build
  steps:
    - script: echo Testing
```

Jobs can be conditionally executed:

```
- job: OptionalJob
  condition: eq(variables['Build.SourceBranchName'], 'main')
```

Steps

Steps are individual tasks or scripts within a job. They can be built-in tasks, scripts, or even custom extensions.

```
steps:
- task: NodeTool@0
  inputs:
    versionSpec: '18.x'

- script: npm install
  displayName: 'Install Dependencies'

- script: npm run lint && npm run test
  displayName: 'Lint and Test'
```

You can also use task inputs for more complex operations:

```
- task: PublishBuildArtifacts@1
  inputs:
    PathtoPublish: 'dist'
    ArtifactName: 'drop'
```

Conditions

Conditions let you control whether a stage, job, or step should run.

Common conditions include:

- `succeeded()`: Only run if previous steps succeeded.

- `failed()`: Only run if previous steps failed.

- `always()`: Run regardless of success or failure.

- `eq()`, `ne()`, `and()`, `or()`: Logical operations.

Example:

```
- script: echo This only runs on main
  condition: eq(variables['Build.SourceBranch'], 'refs/heads/main')
```

Templates

Templates let you reuse and modularize pipeline logic. You can define common steps or jobs in another file.

Step Template:

```
# templates/npm-install.yml
steps:
- script: npm install
```

Main Pipeline:

```
extends:
  template: templates/npm-install.yml
```

Templates support parameters too:

```
# templates/build.yml
parameters:
  - name: config
    default: 'Release'

steps:
- script: dotnet build --configuration ${{ parameters.config }}
```

Parameters

Parameters are more powerful than variables in that they allow type enforcement and are resolved at compile time.

```
parameters:
  - name: environment
    type: string
    default: 'staging'
```

Use in steps:

```
- script: echo Deploying to ${{ parameters.environment }}
```

Matrix and Strategy

Matrix builds allow parallel jobs with different configurations.

```
jobs:
- job: MatrixJob
  strategy:
    matrix:
      linux:
        vmImage: 'ubuntu-latest'
      windows:
        vmImage: 'windows-latest'
  pool:
    vmImage: ${{ matrix.vmImage }}
  steps:
    - script: echo Running on ${{ matrix.vmImage }}
```

This is useful for cross-platform testing or testing multiple versions of a dependency.

Environment and Deployment Jobs

To define environments for deployment:

```
- deployment: DeployWeb
  environment: 'production'
  strategy:
    runOnce:
      deploy:
        steps:
          - script: echo Deploying to production
```

Environments can have:

- Approvals   before   deployment.

- Resource   checks.

- History   of   deployments.

Full Example: Multi-Stage Pipeline

```
trigger:
```

```yaml
  branches:
    include:
      - main

variables:
  buildConfig: 'Release'
  artifactName: 'app'

stages:
- stage: Build
  jobs:
  - job: BuildJob
    pool:
      vmImage: 'ubuntu-latest'
    steps:
    - task: UseDotNet@2
      inputs:
        packageType: 'sdk'
        version: '6.x'
    - script: dotnet build --configuration $(buildConfig)
    - task: PublishBuildArtifacts@1
      inputs:
        pathToPublish: 'bin/Release'
        artifactName: $(artifactName)

- stage: Deploy
  dependsOn: Build
  condition: succeeded()
  jobs:
  - deployment: DeployJob
    environment: 'staging'
    strategy:
      runOnce:
        deploy:
          steps:
          - download: current
            artifact: $(artifactName)
          - script: echo Deploying $(artifactName) to staging
```

Tips for Writing Clean YAML

- **Use consistent indentation**: Always use spaces, not tabs.

- **Keep files short and modular**: Split long pipelines into templates.

- **Name jobs and stages clearly**: Makes logs and dashboards easier to navigate.

- **Comment generously**: YAML doesn't support inline code annotations like scripts — use # liberally to explain intent.

- **Test changes in small increments**: A minor formatting error can break your pipeline entirely.

Conclusion

The YAML syntax and structure for Azure DevOps pipelines enable powerful, maintainable, and automated CI/CD workflows. By mastering these constructs — from simple steps to advanced job strategies, conditional logic, and template reuse — development teams can achieve a high degree of automation, traceability, and scalability. Whether you are managing a simple web app or orchestrating deployments across hundreds of services, the ability to express complex DevOps logic through YAML is a fundamental skill in modern software delivery.

Running and Monitoring Builds

Efficiently running and monitoring builds is at the heart of any successful CI/CD strategy. Azure DevOps provides a powerful and customizable build execution environment combined with robust monitoring tools to ensure reliability, traceability, and visibility across your entire development lifecycle. This section explores the execution model of builds, various ways to run them, the monitoring tools available within Azure DevOps, and how to interpret results, logs, and telemetry for effective debugging and continuous improvement.

Executing Builds: Manual, Triggered, and Scheduled

Azure DevOps pipelines can be executed in several ways, depending on the scenario and stage of development.

Manual Execution

You can manually run a pipeline directly from the Azure DevOps portal. This is particularly useful for one-off tests, hotfixes, or debugging sessions.

Steps to run a pipeline manually:

1. Navigate to **Pipelines > Pipelines** in your Azure DevOps project.

2. Select your pipeline.

3. Click the **Run pipeline** button.

4. Optionally, choose a branch, set variable values, or select a stage to start from.

Manual runs are logged the same way as automated runs, making it easy to compare behaviors.

Automatic Triggering

You can set pipelines to trigger automatically based on changes in the repository.

Example: CI trigger on the main branch:

```
trigger:
  branches:
    include:
      - main
```

You can also trigger pipelines on pull requests, specific file path changes, or tag creation.

Example: Trigger pipeline only when files in the src/ folder change:

```
trigger:
  paths:
    include:
      - src/**
```

Scheduled Builds

For recurring tasks like nightly builds, security scans, or long-running regression tests, schedule-based builds are ideal.

```
schedules:
- cron: "0 1 * * 1-5"  # Every weekday at 1 AM UTC
  displayName: Weekday Nightly Build
  branches:
    include:
      - main
```

Scheduled builds help reduce build congestion during peak hours and enable unattended validation of changes or dependencies.

Monitoring Build Execution

Once a build is initiated, Azure DevOps offers real-time and historical monitoring through the **Runs** interface. The monitoring experience includes:

- **Live console output**: Step-by-step logs appear in real time.

- **Pipeline summary**: A high-level view showing stages and jobs with pass/fail status.

- **Agent assignment**: Identifies which agent ran the pipeline.

- **Duration and performance**: Tracks how long each job or step took.

- **Test and coverage results**: Consolidated view of all test outcomes.

- **Artifact publishing status**: Indicates whether artifacts were successfully produced.

You can access all of these via the **Pipelines > Runs** section, which lists past executions and their results.

Understanding the Logs

Every pipeline run in Azure DevOps generates detailed logs per job, per step. These logs are invaluable for:

- Diagnosing   failures

- Measuring   performance

- Auditing   activities

- Investigating   regressions

Clicking on a failed step expands the error output and shows the standard output and error streams. Logs also provide timestamps for each command and help trace environment variables used during execution.

Example of a log snippet for a failed npm install:

```
2025-04-10T13:45:21.932Z: > npm install
```

```
2025-04-10T13:45:22.004Z: npm ERR! code E404
2025-04-10T13:45:22.005Z:   npm   ERR!   404   Not   Found   -   GET
https://registry.npmjs.org/unknown-package
```

From this, you can immediately identify an issue with a missing or misspelled dependency.

Build Artifacts and Retention

Build artifacts are outputs created during the pipeline process, such as compiled binaries, Docker images, test results, or deployment packages.

To publish artifacts:

```
- task: PublishBuildArtifacts@1
  inputs:
    pathToPublish: 'dist'
    artifactName: 'drop'
```

Azure DevOps stores these artifacts securely, allowing you to:

- Download them manually from the portal
- Use them in a release or deploy stage
- Share them across pipelines

You can configure retention policies to manage storage and automatically delete old artifacts based on age, build status, or tags.

Notifications and Alerts

Azure DevOps provides multiple ways to notify team members of build events:

- **Email alerts** for build failures, completions, or deployments.
- **Service hooks** to integrate with external systems like Slack, Teams, or Jira.
- **Webhooks** for custom integrations.

- **Azure Monitor integration** to push telemetry into dashboards or incident response systems.

To set up a notification:

1. Go to **Project Settings > Notifications**.

2. Choose from built-in subscriptions or create a custom one.

3. Define rules for when and whom to notify.

Using Dashboards for Build Insights

Azure DevOps Dashboards can visualize build performance, failures, and trends. Widgets like **Build History**, **Build Success Rate**, and **Pipeline Duration** give you a birds-eye view of health and throughput.

You can create custom dashboards that highlight:

- Failed builds in the last 7 days

- Average build time by pipeline

- Deployment frequency per environment

These dashboards are shareable and can be set up per project, team, or individual developer.

Test Results and Code Coverage

If your pipeline runs unit or integration tests, Azure DevOps provides native support for collecting and displaying test results and code coverage.

Example task for running tests and publishing results:

```
- script: npm test -- --reporters=jest-junit
- task: PublishTestResults@2
  inputs:
    testResultsFiles: '**/junit.xml'
```

Azure DevOps will:

- Show a summary of passed/failed/skipped tests
- Enable drill-down into test details
- Track test trends over time
- Link failed tests directly to commits and authors

For code coverage:

```
- task: PublishCodeCoverageResults@1
  inputs:
    codeCoverageTool: 'Cobertura'
    summaryFileLocation: 'coverage/cobertura-coverage.xml'
```

The code coverage results are visualized with line-by-line analysis and historical tracking.

Analyzing and Debugging Failures

Builds will fail — that's expected in any active development environment. The key is to react quickly and with clarity. Here's a step-by-step approach to analyzing failed builds:

1. **Identify the failed job or step**.

2. **Read the error logs carefully** — many issues are configuration errors, missing dependencies, or broken tests.

3. **Reproduce locally if needed** to isolate the issue.

4. **Check recent changes** — often failures align with the latest commit.

5. **Use diagnostics settings**, like enabling `system.debug`:

```
variables:
  system.debug: true
```

6. **Use pipeline run comparisons** to contrast successful and failed builds.

Leveraging Analytics for Continuous Improvement

Azure DevOps provides analytics views and Power BI integration for deeper insights. Common KPIs you can track:

- **Build   success   rate**

- **Mean   time   to   recovery   (MTTR)**

- **Build   queue   time**

- **Test   pass   percentage**

- **Lead   time   for   changes**

Improving these metrics over time helps your team deliver software more reliably and predictably.

Example: A Complete CI Build Flow

```
trigger:
  branches:
    include:
      - main

pool:
  vmImage: 'ubuntu-latest'

variables:
  buildConfiguration: 'Release'
  system.debug: true

stages:
- stage: Build
  jobs:
  - job: BuildJob
    steps:
    - task: UseDotNet@2
      inputs:
        packageType: 'sdk'
        version: '6.0.x'
    - script: dotnet restore
    - script: dotnet build --configuration $(buildConfiguration)
    - script: dotnet test --logger:trx
```

```
- task: PublishTestResults@2
  inputs:
    testResultsFiles: '**/*.trx'
- task: PublishBuildArtifacts@1
  inputs:
    pathToPublish: 'bin/Release'
    artifactName: 'app'
```

This pipeline demonstrates the key stages: trigger, restore, build, test, result publishing, and artifact generation — all with visibility into every step.

Conclusion

Running and monitoring builds effectively in Azure DevOps requires a mix of automation discipline and observability tooling. Whether it's a quick hotfix on a Friday or a complex deployment pipeline running dozens of jobs, Azure DevOps equips teams with powerful tools to ensure reliability, traceability, and speed. With build logs, dashboards, test summaries, artifact management, and analytics, teams can confidently ship code — and improve over time.

Mastering this process lays the groundwork for robust continuous delivery, where each commit can be a potential release with minimal manual intervention.

Chapter 4: Building Your First CI Pipeline

Connecting to Source Repositories

Establishing a reliable and secure connection to your source code repository is the first step in building a Continuous Integration (CI) pipeline. Azure DevOps supports multiple source control providers including Azure Repos, GitHub, Bitbucket, and external Git repositories. This flexibility allows teams to use the platform they are most comfortable with or are currently utilizing in their development workflow.

To get started, you'll need to ensure that your project repository is properly configured and accessible. Azure DevOps provides both Git and Team Foundation Version Control (TFVC), but Git is the most commonly used due to its distributed nature and modern tooling support.

Step-by-Step: Connecting Azure Repos

If you are using Azure Repos (Azure DevOps' built-in Git support), follow these steps:

1. Navigate to your Azure DevOps project.

2. Click on **Repos** from the left sidebar.

3. If this is your first time setting up the repository, you can either clone it locally or import an existing repository.

Use the following command to clone the repo locally:

```
git                                                               clone
https://dev.azure.com/yourorganization/yourproject/_git/yourreposito
ry
cd yourrepository
```

4.
5. Once cloned, you can push code changes and monitor history directly within Azure DevOps.

Step-by-Step: Connecting External Git Repositories (e.g., GitHub)

To connect an external Git provider like GitHub:

1. Navigate to **Pipelines** > **Pipelines**.

2. Click **New** pipeline.

3. Choose your repository source (e.g., GitHub).

4. Authenticate with GitHub if you haven't already.

5. Select the desired repository.

6. Azure DevOps will prompt you to configure your pipeline using YAML or the classic editor.

Using GitHub as your source also allows you to leverage GitHub-specific integrations such as GitHub Actions, webhooks, and status checks.

Configuring Repository Settings

Once connected, it's important to configure repository settings such as:

- **Branch Policies**: Enforce standards like pull request reviews and successful builds before merges.

- **Branch Protection Rules**: Especially useful when using GitHub to prevent force pushes and deletion of branches.

- **Service Connections**: Securely store and manage credentials required for external services (e.g., DockerHub, AWS).

These settings help ensure a secure and consistent development process across all team members and environments.

Defining the YAML File for Your Pipeline

With your source repository connected, the next step is to create a YAML pipeline definition. This YAML file describes how Azure DevOps should build your project.

Here's a basic example of a YAML file for a Node.js project:

```
trigger:
  - main

pool:
  vmImage: 'ubuntu-latest'

steps:
  - task: NodeTool@0
```

```
   inputs:
     versionSpec: '16.x'
   displayName: 'Install Node.js'

 - script: |
     npm install
     npm run build
   displayName: 'Install dependencies and build'

 - task: PublishBuildArtifacts@1
   inputs:
     PathtoPublish: 'dist'
     ArtifactName: 'drop'
     publishLocation: 'Container'
```

Let's break down this file:

- **trigger**: Automatically triggers the pipeline when changes are pushed to the main branch.

- **pool**: Specifies the type of agent to run the pipeline on.

- **steps**: Defines tasks such as installing Node.js, building the project, and publishing build   artifacts.

This YAML file should be saved in the root directory of your project, typically named azure-pipelines.yml.

Validating Pipeline Configuration

Once the YAML file is created, it must be validated to ensure correct syntax and logic. Azure DevOps provides built-in validation tools:

1. Navigate   to   **Pipelines**   in   your   project.

2. Click   on   **New**   **pipeline**.

3. Select   the   repository   and   YAML   file.

4. Click   **Run**   to   validate   the   pipeline.

Azure DevOps parses the YAML and initiates the build process. If any syntax errors are present, you'll be notified immediately, allowing you to make corrections.

Use this opportunity to check:

- YAML indentation (very important for correct parsing).

- Correct references to tools or scripts.

- Valid trigger branches and build commands.

Exploring Build Triggers

Build triggers dictate when your CI pipeline is executed. Azure DevOps supports several types:

- **Continuous Integration (CI)**: Triggers on every code push.

- **Scheduled Builds**: Runs at predefined times.

- **Manual Runs**: Allows developers to trigger builds on-demand.

- **Pull Request Validation**: Validates changes before merging.

Here's how you can schedule a build using YAML:

```
schedules:
  - cron: "0 2 * * *"
    displayName: Nightly Build
    branches:
      include:
        - main
    always: true
```

This example schedules a build to run every night at 2:00 AM UTC on the main branch. Scheduled builds are great for running longer tests or generating nightly reports without blocking developer workflows during the day.

Best Practices for Repository Connections in CI

To maximize the reliability of your CI pipeline:

- **Use Service Connections for External Repositories**: This avoids hardcoding tokens or sensitive information.

- **Lock Pipeline Access**: Ensure only authorized team members can edit pipeline configurations.

- **Enable Status Checks on Pull Requests**: Enforce CI success before allowing merges.

- **Keep Dependencies Updated**: Regularly update your build tools and libraries to minimize vulnerabilities.

- **Tag Releases**: Use Git tags and versioning to associate builds with specific releases.

Example: CI Pipeline for Python Application

Here's another example for a Python-based project using Azure Pipelines:

```
trigger:
  - develop

pool:
  vmImage: 'ubuntu-latest'

steps:
  - task: UsePythonVersion@0
    inputs:
      versionSpec: '3.x'
      addToPath: true

  - script: |
      python -m pip install --upgrade pip
      pip install -r requirements.txt
    displayName: 'Install dependencies'

  - script: |
      pytest tests/
    displayName: 'Run tests'

  - task: PublishTestResults@2
    inputs:
```

```
testResultsFormat: 'JUnit'
testResultsFiles: '**/test-results.xml'
```

This pipeline installs Python, dependencies, runs tests using `pytest`, and publishes the results to Azure DevOps.

Version Control for Pipeline Files

Treat your `azure-pipelines.yml` file as part of your source code:

- Keep it under version control.

- Require pull requests for changes.

- Use comments to document each step or configuration.

- Use templates for reusability across multiple projects or services.

For example, common steps like installing dependencies or publishing artifacts can be abstracted into a template file and reused:

```
# azure-pipelines.yml
extends:
  template: templates/base-template.yml
```

This keeps your pipeline files clean and easier to maintain.

Conclusion

Connecting your repository to Azure DevOps is the foundational step in building an effective CI pipeline. Whether using Azure Repos, GitHub, or another Git provider, the goal is the same: enable automated, repeatable builds triggered by code changes. By defining your pipeline in YAML and committing it to source control, you ensure transparency, traceability, and consistency.

In the next section, we will dive into how to create and validate YAML builds, building upon the repository connection established here to craft your first working CI workflow.

Creating and Validating YAML Builds

YAML (YAML Ain't Markup Language) has become the standard format for defining CI/CD pipelines in Azure DevOps. Its simplicity and human-readable structure make it ideal for managing pipeline configurations in source control alongside your code. In this section, we will explore the entire lifecycle of creating and validating YAML builds, from the fundamentals of syntax to debugging and improving complex pipeline definitions.

Why Use YAML for Pipelines?

There are two main ways to create Azure DevOps pipelines: the classic editor (visual designer) and YAML. While the classic editor may seem easier for beginners, YAML offers key advantages:

- **Version control**: YAML files live in your repository, making them easy to audit, version, and collaborate on.

- **Reusability**: Templates and parameterization allow for modular, DRY (Don't Repeat Yourself) pipelines.

- **Transparency**: Every build step is defined clearly, avoiding black-box behavior.

- **Portability**: YAML definitions can be copied across projects and environments with minimal changes.

Basic Structure of a YAML Build Pipeline

Here's the general structure of a simple YAML pipeline:

```
trigger:
  - main

pool:
  vmImage: 'ubuntu-latest'

variables:
  buildConfiguration: 'Release'

steps:
  - script: echo Hello, world!
    displayName: 'Print message'
```

Let's break this down:

- `trigger`: Specifies which branches will trigger the pipeline.

- `pool`: Determines the agent (virtual machine) used to run the pipeline.

- `variables`: Defines custom variables to be used throughout the pipeline.

- `steps`: Contains individual build tasks or scripts.

Step-by-Step Guide to Creating a YAML Build

1. Choose or Create a Repository

Start with a project in Azure DevOps and a Git repository containing your application code. You can either create a new project or use an existing one.

2. Add an `azure-pipelines.yml` File

Create a file in the root directory of your repo named `azure-pipelines.yml`. This is where your build configuration will live. Commit this file to the main branch.

Example content for a .NET project:

```
trigger:
  - main

pool:
  vmImage: 'windows-latest'

variables:
  buildConfiguration: 'Release'

steps:
  - task: UseDotNet@2
    inputs:
      packageType: 'sdk'
      version: '6.0.x'
      installationPath: $(Agent.ToolsDirectory)/dotnet

  - script: dotnet build --configuration $(buildConfiguration)
    displayName: 'Build project'
```

3. Push to Repository

After creating the YAML file, push it to your repository. This push will trigger the pipeline (based on the `trigger` configuration), initiating a build.

Advanced Build Configuration Concepts

Multi-Step Builds

You can add multiple steps to perform various actions:

```
steps:
  - script: npm install
    displayName: 'Install dependencies'

  - script: npm run build
    displayName: 'Build application'

  - script: npm test
    displayName: 'Run tests'
```

Using Predefined Variables

Azure DevOps provides many predefined variables, such as:

- `Build.BuildId`: The unique ID for the build run.

- `Build.SourceBranch`: The name of the branch being built.

- `System.Debug`: Set to `true` for verbose logging.

Example:

```
- script: echo "Running build ID $(Build.BuildId) on branch $(Build.SourceBranch)"
```

Templates for Modularity

To avoid duplicating YAML code across pipelines, use templates:

Template file (`build-template.yml`)

```
parameters:
  - name: buildConfig
    default: 'Release'

steps:
  - script: dotnet build --configuration ${{ parameters.buildConfig
}}
    displayName: 'Build with configuration'
```

Main pipeline file

```
trigger:
  - main

extends:
  template: build-template.yml
  parameters:
    buildConfig: 'Debug'
```

Validating YAML Syntax and Logic

Validation is crucial before relying on a YAML build in production. Azure DevOps offers various validation mechanisms:

1. Pipeline Editor Validation

- Go to **Pipelines** > **New pipeline**.
- Choose your repo and select "YAML".
- Select the `azure-pipelines.yml` file.
- Azure DevOps validates your YAML syntax automatically.
- You'll see syntax errors inline if there are issues.

2. Linting Tools

You can use third-party YAML linters like yamllint to catch formatting issues before pushing:

```
yamllint azure-pipelines.yml
```

This helps identify problems such as inconsistent indentation, duplicate keys, and syntax violations.

3. Manual Validation via Azure CLI

You can simulate pipeline runs using Azure CLI:

```
az pipelines run --name "Your Pipeline Name" --branch main
```

This gives you the flexibility to test different branches and commit states.

Common Errors and How to Fix Them

Incorrect Indentation

YAML is sensitive to indentation. Use spaces, not tabs. Misaligned keys will cause parsing errors.

Incorrect:

```
steps:
 - script: echo "Bad indent"
```

Correct:

```
steps:
  - script: echo "Good indent"
```

Referencing Undefined Variables

Always check variable names and scopes. If a variable doesn't exist, it will be replaced with an empty string.

Fix:

```
variables:
  greeting: 'Hello'

steps:
  - script: echo $(greeting)
```

Missing Required Fields

Tasks may require specific fields. Consult task documentation to ensure correct configuration.

Real-World YAML Pipeline Example (React App)

Here's a complete example for a React-based web application:

```yaml
trigger:
  - main

pool:
  vmImage: 'ubuntu-latest'

variables:
  nodeVersion: '18.x'

steps:
  - task: NodeTool@0
    inputs:
      versionSpec: $(nodeVersion)
    displayName: 'Install Node.js'

  - script: |
      npm install
      npm run build
    displayName: 'Build the React app'

  - task: PublishBuildArtifacts@1
    inputs:
      PathtoPublish: 'build'
      ArtifactName: 'react-app'
      publishLocation: 'Container'
```

This pipeline installs Node.js, installs dependencies, builds the app, and publishes the output folder as a build artifact.

Best Practices for YAML Builds

1. **Keep it simple** – Avoid overly complex logic in YAML. Break down into templates or scripts if necessary.

2. **Use templates** – Reuse common tasks across pipelines to reduce duplication.

3. **Version control everything** – Treat the pipeline as code and enforce pull requests.

4. **Validate locally** – Use linting tools before pushing changes.

5. **Secure sensitive data** – Use Azure Key Vault or pipeline secrets for credentials and tokens.

6. **Modularize pipelines** – Create separate jobs for build, test, and deployment stages.

Debugging Builds

When things go wrong, Azure DevOps provides detailed logs:

- Click on the failed job step.

- Expand the step to see logs.

- Use `System.Debug=true` to increase verbosity.

Example of enabling debug logging:

```
variables:
  System.Debug: true
```

You can also re-run failed jobs, inspect downloaded artifacts, and compare logs across builds to diagnose issues efficiently.

Automating Validation with Pull Requests

Integrate pipeline validation into your development lifecycle by configuring branch policies:

1. Navigate to **Repos** > **Branches**.

2. Click the ellipsis on the `main` branch > **Branch policies**.

3. Add a build validation policy requiring the CI pipeline to succeed before merging.

This ensures that all code meets the build requirements before it's merged into the mainline.

Summary

Creating and validating YAML builds in Azure DevOps is a powerful way to ensure consistency, reliability, and scalability in your CI/CD pipelines. By leveraging YAML's flexibility, integrating it with version control, and enforcing rigorous validation, you build a foundation for a resilient software delivery process.

With a solid YAML pipeline in place, you can iterate quickly, catch issues early, and deploy confidently. The next section will explore how to incorporate build tasks and steps to expand your pipeline's functionality.

Incorporating Build Tasks and Steps

Once your YAML build pipeline is defined and validated, the next critical step is to populate it with meaningful tasks and steps. These represent the actual work your CI pipeline will perform: compiling code, running tests, analyzing quality, creating build artifacts, and more. Azure DevOps provides an extensive catalog of built-in tasks, and you can also write custom scripts or tasks to tailor the pipeline to your specific needs.

This section will explore how to structure and incorporate build steps efficiently, utilize built-in tasks, add conditions and logic, reuse step definitions, and manage dependencies.

Understanding Steps and Tasks

In Azure DevOps, **steps** are the smallest unit of work in a pipeline. A **task** is a predefined piece of functionality (like UseDotNet, PublishBuildArtifacts, DownloadSecureFile), while a **script** step runs inline shell or PowerShell code. Every task or script is a step.

Here's a basic example of a combination of script and task steps:

```
steps:
  - task: NodeTool@0
    inputs:
      versionSpec: '18.x'
    displayName: 'Install Node.js'

  - script: |
      npm install
      npm run build
    displayName: 'Install dependencies and build app'
```

The `NodeTool@0` is a task that installs Node.js, while the `script` step runs shell commands. Both are executed sequentially during the pipeline run.

Using Built-In Tasks

Azure DevOps includes hundreds of prebuilt tasks to simplify common operations such as:

- Building .NET, Java, Node.js, Python applications
- Running tests with popular frameworks
- Uploading and downloading artifacts
- Interacting with Docker, Kubernetes, Azure services

For example, a task for running tests with the `VSTest@2` task:

```
- task: VSTest@2
  inputs:
    testSelector: 'testAssemblies'
    testAssemblyVer2: '**\*test*.dll'
    searchFolder: '$(System.DefaultWorkingDirectory)'
```

The inputs define what to run and where to look. Each task has its own required and optional parameters, documented in Azure DevOps Task Reference.

Customizing Steps with Conditions

You can conditionally run steps based on outcomes of previous steps or defined variables. This is powerful for handling branching logic in your CI process.

Example: Only run the test step if the build step succeeds:

```
- script: dotnet build
  displayName: 'Build project'

- script: dotnet test
  displayName: 'Run tests'
  condition: succeeded()
```

Other useful conditions:

- `always()` — runs regardless of success/failure

- `failed()` — runs only if previous step failed

- `eq(variables['Build.SourceBranch'], 'refs/heads/main')` — branch-specific logic

This fine-grained control ensures your pipeline behaves predictably.

Grouping Tasks into Jobs

You can group steps into **jobs**, which run sequentially or in parallel. This helps separate responsibilities like build vs. test, or platform-specific jobs.

Example:

```
jobs:
  - job: Build
    pool:
      vmImage: 'ubuntu-latest'
    steps:
      - script: echo "Building..."

  - job: Test
    dependsOn: Build
    pool:
      vmImage: 'ubuntu-latest'
    steps:
      - script: echo "Running tests..."
```

Use `dependsOn` to define dependencies between jobs. This allows you to run jobs in parallel or control the flow of execution.

Creating Reusable Steps with Templates

If you find yourself repeating steps across multiple pipelines or jobs, extract them into reusable templates.

Template file (`build-steps.yml`):

```
parameters:
  - name: configuration
    default: 'Release'

steps:
  - script: dotnet restore
    displayName: 'Restore packages'

  - script: dotnet build --configuration ${{ parameters.configuration
}}
    displayName: 'Build project'
```

Main pipeline file:

```
trigger:
  - main

extends:
  template: build-steps.yml
  parameters:
    configuration: 'Debug'
```

Templates help enforce consistency, reduce duplication, and make large pipeline files easier to manage.

Artifact Management in Build Steps

A core function of CI is generating artifacts (e.g., binaries, packages, containers). Use the `PublishBuildArtifacts@1` task to store and pass these artifacts to later stages or releases.

Example:

```
- task: PublishBuildArtifacts@1
  inputs:
    PathtoPublish: 'bin/Release'
    ArtifactName: 'drop'
    publishLocation: 'Container'
```

You can later use `DownloadBuildArtifacts@0` in a deployment job to retrieve the files.

Caching Dependencies

To speed up builds, you can cache dependencies between runs. Azure DevOps supports this with the `Cache@2` task.

Example for caching npm packages:

```
- task: Cache@2
  inputs:
    key: 'npm | "$(Agent.OS)" | package-lock.json'
    restoreKeys: |
      npm | "$(Agent.OS)"
    path: $(Pipeline.Workspace)/.npm
  displayName: Cache NPM packages
```

Caching significantly reduces install times and build durations, especially in large projects.

Build Step for Code Quality

Incorporating code quality and analysis tools into your pipeline ensures healthy codebases.

Example: Using ESLint in a Node.js project:

```
- script: npm run lint
  displayName: 'Run ESLint'
```

For .NET, use static analysis tools like `dotnet-format`, `FxCop`, or integrate SonarQube:

```
- task: SonarQubePrepare@5
  inputs:
    SonarQube: 'YourConnection'
    scannerMode: 'MSBuild'
    projectKey: 'MyProject'

- script: dotnet build
  displayName: 'Build for analysis'

- task: SonarQubeAnalyze@5
```

```
- task: SonarQubePublish@5
```

Creating Secure Steps

Never hardcode secrets in YAML. Use variable groups or Azure Key Vault integration to manage credentials.

```
variables:
  - group: my-secure-group

steps:
  - script: echo $(mySecret)
    displayName: 'Print secret'
```

You can also use `DownloadSecureFile@1` for files like certificates, SSH keys, etc.

Real-World Example: Multi-Platform Build

Imagine a cross-platform project that needs to be built for Windows and Linux:

```
jobs:
  - job: Build_Windows
    pool:
      vmImage: 'windows-latest'
    steps:
      - script: build-windows.sh
        displayName: 'Build on Windows'

  - job: Build_Linux
    pool:
      vmImage: 'ubuntu-latest'
    steps:
      - script: build-linux.sh
        displayName: 'Build on Linux'
```

These jobs will execute in parallel, improving efficiency and ensuring platform compatibility.

Organizing Large Pipelines

For large pipelines, adopt these organizational tips:

- **Break into multiple files** using `include`, `extends`, and templates.

- **Use parameterized jobs** to run matrix builds (e.g., test multiple Node.js versions).

- **Comment generously** to explain complex logic.

- **Segment logically**: separate build, test, packaging, and deployment.

Summary

Incorporating build tasks and steps is where your YAML pipeline comes to life. This is the stage where actual code transformation, verification, packaging, and reporting happen. Azure DevOps' rich task ecosystem and flexible YAML syntax allow you to orchestrate everything from a simple build to a complex, cross-platform, policy-enforced pipeline.

As your projects scale, remember to keep your pipelines clean, modular, and secure. Up next, we'll dive into executing and monitoring these builds, so you can verify everything's working and troubleshoot quickly when it's not.

Running and Monitoring Builds

Running and monitoring builds is the operational phase of your CI pipeline—where automation meets execution. Once your pipeline is defined, and build tasks are configured, the next step is triggering it, observing its behavior, interpreting logs, responding to failures, and integrating feedback mechanisms. Azure DevOps provides powerful tools to manage builds across projects, branches, teams, and environments.

In this section, we'll walk through manual and automated triggers, real-time monitoring, interpreting build logs, using analytics, handling failures, and integrating notifications to keep your team informed.

Triggering Builds

There are several ways to trigger a build in Azure DevOps:

1. Automatic Triggers

These are defined in your `azure-pipelines.yml` file using the `trigger` keyword:

```
trigger:
  - main
```

This runs the pipeline every time a commit is pushed to the main branch.

You can also use more advanced options like path filters:

```
trigger:
  branches:
    include:
      - main
  paths:
    include:
      - src/*
    exclude:
      - docs/*
```

This runs the build only when files in the src/ folder change, avoiding unnecessary builds.

2. Manual Trigger (Run Pipeline)

In the Azure DevOps UI:

- Navigate to **Pipelines** > **Pipelines**
- Click your pipeline
- Click **Run** **pipeline**
- Choose a branch, specify variables, and click **Run**

This is useful for ad hoc builds, testing changes, or verifying branches before PRs.

3. Scheduled Builds

To run builds at specific times (e.g., nightly), use schedules:

```
schedules:
  - cron: "0 3 * * *"
    displayName: Nightly Build
    branches:
      include:
        - main
```

```
always: true
```

This example runs at 3:00 AM UTC every day. Scheduled builds are perfect for long-running tasks like performance testing, security scanning, or building documentation.

Real-Time Monitoring

Once a build is running, Azure DevOps offers a live build console to monitor progress.

Viewing Running Builds:

- Go to **Pipelines** > **Runs**
- Click on the latest build run
- The UI shows:
  - Summary view (status, duration, trigger info)
  - Logs for each step
  - Timeline with jobs and phases
  - Associated commits, pull requests, and work items

Logs update in real time, giving you visibility into what's happening behind the scenes. Each job and step can be expanded to show detailed output, including environment setup, task execution, and script outputs.

Interpreting Logs

Effective log reading is essential for debugging and optimization.

Key Elements in Build Logs:

- **Initialization** – Agent provisioning, environment setup
- **Dependency resolution** – E.g., package installs
- **Build output** – Compilation results, warnings, errors
- **Test results** – Pass/fail information, tracebacks

- **Artifacts** – Upload confirmation and paths

- **Summary** – Exit codes, step durations, total time

Improving Log Readability

Use echo statements in your scripts:

```
- script: |
    echo "Installing dependencies..."
    npm install
```

For long builds, separate steps clearly:

```
- script: |
    echo "=================="
    echo "BUILD STARTED"
    echo "=================="
```

You can also set the verbosity level using:

```
variables:
  System.Debug: true
```

This produces detailed agent output, useful for tracking variable values and execution paths.

Handling Failures

Build failures are expected during development. The goal is to diagnose and fix them quickly.

Common Failure Scenarios:

- **Dependency failures** – Incorrect or missing packages

- **Syntax errors** – Code issues causing build scripts to break

- **Environment mismatches** – Platform-specific bugs or incompatible versions

- **Failing tests** – Code regressions

- **Timeouts** – Long-running steps exceeding limits

Steps to Diagnose:

1. Identify the failed step in the logs.

2. Read the error message and trace back to the script line or task input.

3. Check recent commits for changes.

4. Verify environment settings (Node version, SDK versions, etc.).

5. If using variables or templates, ensure they resolve correctly.

Rerunning Builds

Use the **Rerun failed jobs** or **Rerun entire pipeline** buttons. If the failure was transient (e.g., network issue), the rerun might succeed without changes.

Analyzing Build Metrics

Azure DevOps includes analytics features to identify trends and bottlenecks:

- **Build duration** – Track time for each phase and step
- **Success/failure rates** – Identify flaky tests or unstable environments
- **Test coverage** – If integrated with testing tools
- **Agent utilization** – Determine if more agents are needed

You can access these metrics in:

- **Pipelines > Analytics views**
- **Dashboards** using the **Build Metrics widget**
- **Power BI** (via Azure DevOps data connectors)

Custom metrics can also be written to logs or published as artifacts and then analyzed downstream.

Notifying the Team

Effective CI involves rapid feedback. Azure DevOps supports several notification methods:

1. Email Notifications

- Navigate to **Project Settings > Notifications**
- Set up rules for:
  - Build success/failure
  - Pull request updates
  - Build completion for specific branches

Example: Notify developers only on failure:

```
- script: echo "Build failed!"
  condition: failed()
```

2. Teams/Slack Integration

Azure DevOps supports direct integration with Microsoft Teams and Slack.

- Go to **Project Settings > Service Hooks**
- Choose your messaging platform
- Configure trigger (e.g., build failed on main branch)
- Add webhook to post notifications to the appropriate channel

3. Custom Webhooks

Use custom service hooks to integrate with third-party tools like PagerDuty, JIRA, or Discord.

Pipeline Logs and Retention

By default, Azure DevOps retains build logs and artifacts for 30 days. You can customize retention in pipeline settings:

- **Keep forever** – Prevents logs from being auto-deleted.
- **Retention policy** – Set shorter or longer retention based on pipeline type.

Use this YAML to retain builds indefinitely:

```yaml
- task: PublishBuildArtifacts@1
  inputs:
    PathtoPublish: 'dist'
    ArtifactName: 'drop'
    publishLocation: 'Container'
  retention:
    days: 0
    minimumToKeep: 1
```

Build Artifacts Access

Once a build is successful, artifacts are available in the **Summary** tab.

Steps to download:

1. Go to **Pipelines** > **Runs**
2. Click the completed build
3. Select **Artifacts** on the right
4. Download or browse the published files

Artifacts can also be passed to release pipelines or deployed automatically using deployment jobs.

Pipeline Run Approvals

For sensitive environments (e.g., production), you can configure **environment approvals**:

- Go to **Pipelines** > **Environments**
- Add an environment (e.g., "Production")
- Set required reviewers before deployments proceed

This integrates with the build pipeline using deployment jobs:

```yaml
jobs:
- deployment: DeployToProd
```

```
environment: 'Production'
strategy:
  runOnce:
    deploy:
      steps:
        - script: echo "Deploying to Production"
```

When the build reaches this job, Azure DevOps will pause and wait for approval.

Cleaning Up Build Outputs

To avoid bloated storage usage, implement clean-up tasks:

- Delete intermediate files after packaging

- Use `.gitignore` to avoid pushing unnecessary files

- Use pipeline caching rather than artifacts for dependencies

Example:

```
- script: rm -rf node_modules dist tmp
  displayName: 'Clean up workspace'
```

Best Practices for Running and Monitoring Builds

- **Fail fast** – Put quick validation steps early to catch errors before expensive steps.

- **Use test summaries** – Include pass/fail counts, durations, and links to logs.

- **Color-code logs** – Use ANSI codes for colored output in supported terminals.

- **Separate long-running steps** – Use parallel jobs or scheduled builds.

- **Set timeouts** – Prevent jobs from hanging indefinitely:

```
jobs:
- job: Build
  timeoutInMinutes: 20
  steps:
```

```
- script: npm run build
```

Summary

Running and monitoring builds is more than just hitting a button—it's about creating a transparent, informative feedback loop that supports rapid development and reliable delivery. Azure DevOps gives you powerful tools to trigger builds automatically or manually, monitor progress, inspect results, recover from failures, and continuously improve based on insights.

By implementing thoughtful monitoring, clear logs, meaningful alerts, and metrics-driven iteration, you ensure that your CI pipeline becomes a strategic asset in your software delivery lifecycle. In the next chapter, we'll explore how to take these builds and turn them into continuous deployment pipelines that ship your product to users with confidence.

Chapter 5. Advanced CI Techniques

Multi-Stage and Conditional Builds

Multi-stage and conditional builds are powerful features in Azure DevOps Pipelines that enable teams to define complex build workflows in a structured, maintainable, and reusable format. These capabilities support cleaner pipeline organization, allow conditional logic to tailor execution paths, and facilitate artifact reuse and stage-level control.

Understanding Multi-Stage Pipelines

A multi-stage pipeline allows you to divide your CI process into distinct logical stages. For example, you may define separate stages for building, testing, and packaging your application. This modularity promotes reusability, clearer error identification, and better orchestration.

Each stage can consist of one or more jobs, and each job can include multiple steps. Azure DevOps executes stages sequentially by default, but with dependencies and conditions, you can customize the execution flow.

Basic Multi-Stage Pipeline Structure

Here's an example of a simple multi-stage YAML pipeline:

```yaml
trigger:
  branches:
    include:
      - main

stages:
  - stage: Build
    jobs:
      - job: BuildJob
        pool:
          vmImage: 'ubuntu-latest'
        steps:
          - task: DotNetCoreCLI@2
            inputs:
              command: 'build'
              projects: '**/*.csproj'

  - stage: Test
    dependsOn: Build
    jobs:
      - job: TestJob
```

```
        pool:
          vmImage: 'ubuntu-latest'
        steps:
          - task: DotNetCoreCLI@2
            inputs:
              command: 'test'
              projects: '**/*Tests.csproj'

  - stage: Package
    dependsOn: Test
    condition: succeeded()
    jobs:
      - job: PackageJob
        pool:
          vmImage: 'ubuntu-latest'
        steps:
          - task: DotNetCoreCLI@2
            inputs:
              command: 'publish'
              publishWebProjects: true
              zipAfterPublish: true
```

In this example:

- The `Build` stage compiles the code.

- The `Test` stage runs unit tests.

- The `Package` stage packages the build output, but only if the `Test` stage is successful.

Benefits of Multi-Stage Pipelines

1. **Clarity and Maintainability**
   Large pipelines are easier to manage when divided into stages. Each stage can focus on a single aspect of the pipeline process.

2. **Error Isolation**
   Failures are easier to debug because they are isolated to specific stages.

3. **Incremental Progress**
   If earlier stages succeed, they can generate artifacts that subsequent stages

consume,   reducing   duplication   and   unnecessary   reruns.

4. **Deployment**   **Integration**
   You can integrate both CI and CD in a single YAML file, allowing for end-to-end automation.

Conditional Execution

Azure DevOps allows defining conditional logic to control whether stages, jobs, or steps should run. Conditions are based on expressions evaluated at runtime, often relying on build outcomes, branch filters, variable states, or custom logic.

Built-in Conditions

- `succeeded()` – Executes if the previous stage/job succeeded.

- `failed()` – Executes if the previous stage/job failed.

- `always()` – Executes regardless of success or failure.

- `canceled()` – Executes only if the pipeline run was canceled.

You can also write custom conditions using expressions.

Example: Conditional Stage

```
- stage: Deploy
  dependsOn: Package
  condition:    and(succeeded(),    eq(variables['Build.SourceBranch'],
'refs/heads/main'))
  jobs:
    - job: DeployJob
      steps:
        - script: echo "Deploying to production..."
```

In this example, the `Deploy` stage will only run if the pipeline is successful **and** the source branch is `main`.

Using Runtime and Template Expressions

Azure DevOps supports two types of expressions for conditionals:

1. **Runtime Expressions** ($[...]$)
   Evaluated when the pipeline runs. Useful for accessing variables dynamically.

2. **Template Expressions** (${{ }})
   Evaluated during the compilation of the pipeline YAML. Typically used in reusable templates.

Example: Runtime Expression

```
- script: echo "This runs only if a variable is true"
  condition: eq(variables['runDeploy'], 'true')
```

Example: Template Expression in a Parameter

```
parameters:
  - name: buildConfiguration
    type: string
    default: 'Release'

jobs:
  - job: Build
    steps:
      - script: echo "Building with config ${{ parameters.buildConfiguration }}"
```

Implementing Custom Conditions

You can set custom conditions for more granular control. For example, to skip a stage if a specific file hasn't changed:

```
- stage: Docs
  condition: |
    or(
      startsWith(variables['Build.SourceBranch'],
'refs/heads/docs'),
      changesetContains('docs/**')
    )
  jobs:
    - job: DocsBuild
      steps:
        - script: echo "Building docs..."
```

Although `changesetContains` isn't natively supported, you can achieve similar functionality using third-party extensions or scripts that analyze the Git diff.

Stage and Job Dependencies

You can control the flow of your pipeline using `dependsOn`. By default, each stage depends on the previous one. But you can override this to create parallel or customized flows.

Example: Parallel Execution

```
stages:
  - stage: Build
    jobs:
      - job: BuildApp

  - stage: Lint
    dependsOn: []
    jobs:
      - job: RunLint

  - stage: SecurityScan
    dependsOn: []
    jobs:
      - job: ScanJob
```

Here, `Lint` and `SecurityScan` run independently of `Build`.

Combining Conditions and Variables

Azure DevOps supports using both predefined and custom variables in conditions, providing flexibility in pipeline control.

Example: Branch-Based Execution

```
- job: DeployStaging
  condition:                                        and(succeeded(),
eq(variables['Build.SourceBranchName'], 'develop'))

- job: DeployProduction
  condition:                                        and(succeeded(),
eq(variables['Build.SourceBranchName'], 'main'))
```

This setup ensures that staging and production deployments only occur on their respective branches.

Multi-Stage Templates

To enhance maintainability, especially in enterprise-scale pipelines, define stages as templates and reuse them across projects.

Example Template File (`build-stage.yml`)

```yaml
parameters:
  - name: projectName
    type: string

stages:
  - stage: Build
    jobs:
      - job: BuildJob
        steps:
          - script: echo "Building project ${{ parameters.projectName
}}"
```

Using the Template

```yaml
stages:
  - template: build-stage.yml
    parameters:
      projectName: MyApp
```

Best Practices for Multi-Stage and Conditional Builds

1. **Fail Fast**: Put critical tests and validations early in the pipeline to catch issues quickly.

2. **Reuse Templates**: Use templates to promote DRY (Don't Repeat Yourself) principles and standardization.

3. **Use Descriptive Names**: Stage and job names should clearly communicate their purpose.

4. **Control Access**: Apply stage-level approvals and checks where sensitive operations are involved.

5. **Leverage Caching**: Cache dependencies (e.g., `npm`, `pip`) between runs to speed up builds.

6. **Enforce Policies**: Use branch filters and environment protections to guard against accidental   changes.

Conclusion

Multi-stage and conditional builds are essential tools for implementing scalable, maintainable, and robust CI workflows. With YAML pipelines in Azure DevOps, teams can fine-tune execution logic, promote code reuse, and clearly structure their CI pipeline across various stages. When used effectively, these techniques reduce build time, increase pipeline reliability, and enable complex delivery patterns—all critical components of a mature DevOps strategy.

Build Artifact Management

Effective artifact management is a cornerstone of modern CI/CD pipelines. Artifacts represent the outputs of your build process—binaries, compiled code, packages, configuration files, logs, or any other deliverable that must be preserved and possibly transferred across stages or deployed. In Azure DevOps, managing these artifacts efficiently ensures consistency across environments, enables traceability, and improves the scalability of deployments.

What Are Build Artifacts?

In Azure DevOps Pipelines, a **build artifact** is any file or set of files produced during a pipeline run that you want to make available for use in later stages or by other pipelines. These artifacts are stored in Azure DevOps and can be accessed from the pipeline summary, shared across stages, or downloaded by external tools or users.

Common examples include:

- .NET `.dll` or `.nupkg` files

- Java `.jar` or `.war` files

- Web assets (HTML, CSS, JS bundles)

- Docker images (managed differently)

- Configuration files

- Test reports and coverage data

Creating and Publishing Artifacts

Azure Pipelines provides the `PublishBuildArtifacts@1` task to explicitly publish artifacts at the end of a job. You can define multiple artifact outputs, and each can be named and stored separately.

Example: Publishing Artifacts

```
steps:
  - task: CopyFiles@2
    inputs:
      SourceFolder: '$(Build.ArtifactStagingDirectory)'
      Contents: '**'
      TargetFolder: '$(Build.ArtifactStagingDirectory)/drop'

  - task: PublishBuildArtifacts@1
    inputs:
      PathtoPublish: '$(Build.ArtifactStagingDirectory)/drop'
      ArtifactName: 'drop'
      publishLocation: 'Container'
```

In this example:

- `CopyFiles@2` prepares the files for publishing.

- `PublishBuildArtifacts@1` uploads the `drop` folder as a build artifact.

You can view these artifacts in the Azure DevOps UI under the pipeline run details and download them if needed.

Consuming Artifacts in Subsequent Stages

When using multi-stage YAML pipelines, you can automatically pass artifacts from one stage to another using implicit sharing. However, if you need finer control—such as reusing artifacts from a different pipeline—you can use the `DownloadBuildArtifacts@0` task.

Example: Consuming Artifacts from Previous Stage

```
- stage: Deploy
  dependsOn: Build
  jobs:
    - job: DeployJob
```

```
steps:
  - download: current
    artifact: drop

  - script: |
      ls $(Pipeline.Workspace)/drop
      echo "Deploying from artifact..."
```

Here, `download: current` fetches the artifacts produced by earlier stages in the same pipeline.

Example: Downloading Artifacts from a Different Pipeline

```
- task: DownloadBuildArtifacts@0
  inputs:
    buildType: 'specific'
    project: 'MyProject'
    pipeline: 42
    buildVersionToDownload: 'latest'
    downloadPath: '$(Pipeline.Workspace)/external'
```

This approach is useful for scenarios where you maintain a separate pipeline for builds and want to reference its outputs in a different release or deployment pipeline.

Artifact Storage and Retention

Azure DevOps stores artifacts in an internal container by default. You can configure the retention policy on the pipeline or organization level to control how long these artifacts are kept.

Retention Policy Settings:

- **Days to retain artifacts**: Define how long Azure DevOps should keep the artifacts.

- **Keep artifacts from the latest successful builds only**: Useful to avoid accumulation.

- **Manually retained builds**: These are exempt from cleanup unless manually deleted.

To configure retention, navigate to:

Project Settings → Pipelines → Settings → Retention

Artifact Naming and Organization

Good artifact naming conventions help maintain clarity and traceability, especially in large-scale CI/CD systems.

Best practices:

- Use descriptive artifact names (e.g., `backend-build`, `web-assets`, `infrastructure-scripts`).

- Include metadata like build version or branch name inside the files or paths.

- Maintain consistent folder structures across stages.

Example:

```
- task: PublishBuildArtifacts@1
  inputs:
    PathtoPublish: '$(Build.ArtifactStagingDirectory)/dist'
    ArtifactName: 'web-assets'
```

Artifact Sharing Across Pipelines

Azure DevOps supports linking artifacts across pipelines to enable modular design and reduce redundant work.

Pipeline Resources

Use the `resources` keyword to declare another pipeline as a dependency.

```
resources:
  pipelines:
    - pipeline: sharedBuild
      source: SharedProject-CI
      trigger:
        branches:
          include:
            - main

stages:
  - stage: Deploy
    jobs:
```

```
- job: DeployJob
  steps:
    - download: sharedBuild
      artifact: drop
```

This allows your current pipeline to automatically consume artifacts from the `SharedProject-CI` pipeline when it completes.

Working with Universal Packages

For structured package management, Azure DevOps supports **Universal Packages**, which are artifact types that can be versioned and managed via Azure Artifacts.

Uploading a Universal Package

You can use the `AzureCLI@2` task or `AzureArtifactsToolInstaller@1` to work with packages.

```
- task: AzureCLI@2
  inputs:
    azureSubscription: 'MyServiceConnection'
    scriptType: 'bash'
    scriptLocation: 'inlineScript'
    inlineScript: |
      az artifacts universal publish \
        --organization "https://dev.azure.com/myorg" \
        --feed "myfeed" \
        --name "mypackage" \
        --version "1.0.0" \
        --description "My universal package" \
        --path "$(Build.ArtifactStagingDirectory)/output"
```

Universal Packages are ideal for sharing artifacts across multiple teams and projects in a structured, version-controlled way.

Artifact Versioning

Versioning is crucial to ensure consistency and traceability. Common strategies include:

- Using build numbers ($(Build.BuildNumber))

- Including Git commit SHAs ($(Build.SourceVersion))

- Tagging based on semantic versioning

Example:
```
variables:
  version: '1.0.$(Build.BuildId)'

steps:
  - script: echo "##vso[build.updatebuildnumber]$(version)"
```

This sets the build number to something like `1.0.1023`, which can then be used in your artifacts, packages, or deployment paths.

Accessing Artifacts via REST API

Azure DevOps exposes REST APIs to programmatically access build artifacts. This is useful for external automation, integrations, or custom tooling.

Example: Get Artifacts from a Build
```
GET
https://dev.azure.com/{organization}/{project}/_apis/build/builds/{buildId}/artifacts?api-version=7.1-preview.5
```

You'll need a personal access token (PAT) with the appropriate permissions.

Cleaning Up and Retaining Specific Artifacts

You can use build tags and retention settings to control which artifacts are retained longer.

Tagging Builds for Retention
```
- script: echo "##vso[build.addbuildtag]keep"
```

You can then set retention policies to keep builds with specific tags while cleaning up others regularly.

Best Practices for Artifact Management

1. **Keep**   **Artifacts**   **Small**
   Avoid storing large files unnecessarily. Only publish what's needed for downstream stages or deployments.

2. **Avoid**   **Sensitive**   **Data**
   Never include secrets or sensitive configuration files in artifacts. Use Azure Key Vault or secure variables instead.

3. **Use**   **Consistent**   **Paths**   **and**   **Structures**
   Standardized artifact structures simplify reuse and scripting.

4. **Automate**   **Cleanup**
   Set retention policies or use scripts to clean up stale or unused artifacts regularly.

5. **Secure**   **Downloads**
   Use scoped access tokens or service connections when downloading artifacts outside of Azure DevOps.

6. **Enable**   **Traceability**
   Include metadata (like version, commit, author) in artifact contents or names.

Conclusion

Build artifact management is a foundational part of an efficient CI/CD pipeline in Azure DevOps. Whether you're working on small applications or managing enterprise-scale deployments, a well-structured artifact strategy improves traceability, enhances performance, and facilitates seamless promotion of builds across environments.

By leveraging built-in tasks like `PublishBuildArtifacts`, `DownloadBuildArtifacts`, and pipeline resources, along with adopting best practices around retention, naming, and versioning, you can ensure a robust, scalable artifact management process that supports continuous integration and delivery with confidence.

Integrating Static Code Analysis and Tests

Static code analysis and automated testing are critical components of a robust CI pipeline. They allow development teams to catch issues early, enforce coding standards, and ensure that changes do not introduce regressions. Azure DevOps makes it simple to integrate these practices into your CI workflows using built-in tasks, marketplace extensions, and custom scripts.

The goal of this section is to walk you through the principles and practical implementation of static code analysis and automated testing in Azure DevOps pipelines. We'll cover language-specific tooling, best practices, code quality gates, and reporting mechanisms that help teams maintain high standards in software delivery.

The Importance of Static Analysis and Testing

Static Code Analysis refers to the process of evaluating source code without executing it. Tools analyze code structure, formatting, potential bugs, security vulnerabilities, and code smells.

Automated Testing includes unit, integration, and end-to-end tests that validate software functionality. Running these tests as part of the CI pipeline ensures that defects are identified before they reach production.

Together, these practices help:

- Improve code quality and maintainability

- Enforce team or organizational standards

- Prevent regressions and bugs

- Reduce technical debt over time

- Provide rapid feedback to developers

Static Code Analysis Tools

Azure DevOps supports a wide range of static analysis tools for different languages, including:

- **.NET**: Roslyn Analyzers, StyleCop, FxCop, SonarQube

- **Java**: PMD, Checkstyle, FindBugs, SonarQube

- **JavaScript/TypeScript**: ESLint, TSLint (deprecated), Prettier

- **Python**: Pylint, Flake8, Bandit

- **C++**: Cppcheck, Clang-Tidy

- **Go**: GolangCI-Lint

These tools can be run in the pipeline using scripts, tasks, or Docker containers.

Example: Integrating ESLint for a Node.js Project

```
steps:
  - script: |
      npm install
      npm run lint
    displayName: 'Run ESLint'
```

Ensure that your `package.json` includes a `lint` script:

```
"scripts": {
  "lint": "eslint . --ext .js,.ts"
}
```

Incorporating Code Analysis in YAML Pipelines

You can run analysis tools as part of your build jobs using command-line scripts or built-in tasks.

Example: .NET Static Analysis

```
steps:
  - task: DotNetCoreCLI@2
    inputs:
      command: 'build'
      projects: '**/*.csproj'

  - script: dotnet format --verify-no-changes
    displayName: 'Run Code Formatter'

  - script: dotnet build --no-incremental /warnaserror
    displayName: 'Build with Warnings as Errors'
```

Using `/warnaserror` enforces that all warnings are treated as build-breaking errors, improving discipline in code quality.

SonarQube and SonarCloud Integration

SonarQube and **SonarCloud** are popular tools for deep static analysis, providing metrics like code coverage, duplications, code smells, complexity, and security vulnerabilities.

Azure DevOps has direct integration support via marketplace extensions.

Steps to Use SonarCloud in Azure DevOps

1. Install the **SonarCloud** extension from the marketplace.

2. Create a SonarCloud project and generate a token.

3. Add the following tasks in your pipeline:

```
steps:
  - task: SonarCloudPrepare@1
    inputs:
      SonarCloud: 'SonarCloudConnection'
      organization: 'my-org'
      scannerMode: 'MSBuild'
      projectKey: 'myproject'
      projectName: 'MyProject'

  - task: DotNetCoreCLI@2
    inputs:
      command: 'build'
      projects: '**/*.csproj'

  - task: SonarCloudAnalyze@1

  - task: SonarCloudPublish@1
    inputs:
      pollingTimeoutSec: '300'
```

This integration will upload analysis results to SonarCloud, where you can review them in a visual dashboard.

Unit Testing in Pipelines

Unit tests validate isolated units of code (e.g., functions or classes). Azure DevOps supports test runners for various languages:

- **.NET:** MSTest, xUnit, NUnit

- **Java:** JUnit, TestNG

- **JavaScript/TypeScript:** Jest, Mocha

- **Python:** unittest, pytest

- **Go:** go test

Example: Running .NET Tests

```
steps:
  - task: DotNetCoreCLI@2
    inputs:
      command: 'test'
      projects: '**/*Tests.csproj'
      arguments: '--logger trx'
```

You can then publish the results:

```
- task: PublishTestResults@2
  inputs:
    testResultsFormat: 'VSTest'
    testResultsFiles: '**/*.trx'
    failTaskOnFailedTests: true
```

Coverage Reporting

Test coverage measures how much of your codebase is exercised by tests. High coverage is not a guarantee of quality, but low coverage is a warning sign.

Example: Collecting Code Coverage for .NET

```
- task: DotNetCoreCLI@2
  inputs:
    command: 'test'
    projects: '**/*Tests.csproj'
    arguments: '--collect:"XPlat Code Coverage"'
```

Then publish it:

```
- task: PublishCodeCoverageResults@1
```

```
  inputs:
    codeCoverageTool: 'cobertura'
    summaryFileLocation:
'$(Agent.TempDirectory)/**/coverage.cobertura.xml'
```

Coverage results will be displayed in Azure DevOps's Test tab.

Running Tests for JavaScript Projects

Jest Example

Ensure jest and the jest-junit reporter are installed, and your package.json includes:

```
"scripts": {
  "test": "jest --ci --reporters=default --reporters=jest-junit"
}
```

Then in your pipeline:

```
steps:
  - script: npm install
    displayName: 'Install Dependencies'

  - script: npm test
    displayName: 'Run Tests'

  - task: PublishTestResults@2
    inputs:
      testResultsFiles: '**/junit.xml'
      testResultsFormat: 'JUnit'
```

Using Conditional Testing

Sometimes, you want to run different test suites depending on the branch, environment, or other variables.

Example: Run Tests Only on Main Branch

```
- script: npm test
  condition: eq(variables['Build.SourceBranch'], 'refs/heads/main')
```

This ensures that heavier or slower test suites only run when needed.

Integrating Linting and Formatting

Linters catch issues like unused variables, style mismatches, or suspicious logic. Formatters ensure consistent code appearance.

Recommended approach:

- Run   linters   before   tests
- Fail   the   build   if   linting   fails
- Auto-fix   where   possible   in   local   development

```
- script: npm run lint
  displayName: 'Run ESLint'

- script: npx prettier --check .
  displayName: 'Check Prettier Formatting'
```

Test and Analysis Dashboards

Azure DevOps provides dashboards to visualize:

- Passed/failed   tests   over   time
- Code   coverage   trends
- Warnings   and   errors   from   static   analysis
- Build   failures   and   durations

Create custom widgets to monitor quality metrics as part of your DevOps health indicators.

Best Practices for Static Analysis and Testing

1. **Shift Left**: Run analysis and tests early in the pipeline to catch issues fast.

2. **Fail Fast**: Abort builds early if code quality or tests fail.

3. **Enforce Thresholds**: Require minimum coverage, zero critical code smells, or all linters to pass.

4. **Use Templates**: Reuse common testing/linting steps across projects.

5. **Gate Releases**: Prevent deployment if critical bugs or failing tests exist.

6. **Integrate IDE Tools**: Developers should get feedback before code reaches CI.

7. **Automate Everything**: Make it easy to run the same checks locally and in CI.

8. **Measure Over Time**: Use dashboards to track progress on coverage and quality metrics.

Conclusion

Static code analysis and automated testing are indispensable to building resilient, maintainable software. In Azure DevOps, incorporating these into your CI pipelines ensures that every commit meets a consistent standard of quality. By running linters, code formatters, security scanners, unit tests, and coverage tools directly in your build process, you create a development environment where issues are caught early, fixes are faster, and the cost of quality is minimized.

Optimizing Build Performance

Optimizing build performance is crucial for maintaining developer productivity, speeding up feedback cycles, and reducing infrastructure costs. In CI/CD pipelines, slow builds lead to longer feedback loops, reduced release velocity, and frustration across development teams. Azure DevOps offers various tools, settings, and techniques to streamline builds and reduce unnecessary overhead.

This section explores strategies and best practices for optimizing build pipelines in Azure DevOps, covering build parallelization, caching, incremental builds, pipeline efficiency, and infrastructure choices.

Diagnosing Build Performance Bottlenecks

Before optimizing, it's essential to understand where bottlenecks occur. Azure DevOps provides insights through:

- **Build logs**: Step-level timestamps highlight slow stages.

- **Pipeline analytics**: Summary views reveal trends over time.

- **Custom telemetry**: Custom scripts can capture granular metrics.

Key metrics to monitor:

- Time spent on dependency installation

- Build and test execution time

- Artifact publishing duration

- Queue times and agent provisioning delays

Example: Analyzing Logs

Each pipeline step logs start and finish times. Use these to identify stages that take disproportionately long. If `npm install` takes 3–5 minutes in every run, it's a candidate for caching.

Leveraging Pipeline Caching

Caching is one of the most effective ways to reduce build time, particularly when dealing with large dependencies or tools.

Azure Pipelines supports a native `Cache@2` task for caching files between runs. This is ideal for package managers (e.g., `npm`, `pip`, `nuget`) or compiled build artifacts.

Example: Caching npm Packages

```
- task: Cache@2
  inputs:
    key: 'npm | "$(Agent.OS)" | package-lock.json'
    restoreKeys: |
      npm | "$(Agent.OS)"
    path: ~/.npm
  displayName: 'Cache npm packages'
```

In this example, the cache key is tied to the `package-lock.json` file. If dependencies haven't changed, npm packages are restored from the cache, saving significant time.

Other Common Cache Use Cases

- Python   virtual   environments

- Maven/Gradle   .m2   repositories

- NuGet   packages

- Docker   image   layers

- Node   modules   and   Yarn   caches

Reducing Dependency Installation Time

Dependency management often causes the longest delays in CI pipelines. Some strategies to reduce this overhead:

1. **Pin versions**: Avoid dependency resolution issues by pinning specific versions in lock files.

2. **Use lock files**: `package-lock.json`, `Pipfile.lock`, and `packages.lock.json` speed up dependency resolution.

3. **Enable parallel downloads**: Tools like `pip` and `npm` support concurrent fetching.

4. **Use hosted feeds**: Use Azure Artifacts or a private registry for faster and secure dependency retrieval.

Enabling Incremental Builds

Incremental builds reuse outputs from previous builds when code hasn't changed. This dramatically reduces compile times.

.NET Projects: Use the `/incremental` flag or enable it in `csproj`.

```
<IncrementalBuild>true</IncrementalBuild>
```

C++ Projects: Leverage object file reuse and dependency tracking with tools like `ccache`.

JavaScript Projects: Tools like `Webpack` and `esbuild` support incremental builds via persistent caching.

YAML Strategy for .NET

```
- task: DotNetCoreCLI@2
  inputs:
    command: 'build'
    arguments: '--no-restore --no-dependencies'
```

This skips unnecessary restore or dependency re-evaluation steps.

Using Parallel Jobs and Matrix Builds

Azure Pipelines supports running multiple jobs in parallel to take advantage of available agents.

Example: Parallel Test Matrix

```
strategy:
  matrix:
    linux:
      imageName: 'ubuntu-latest'
    windows:
      imageName: 'windows-latest'
    mac:
      imageName: 'macos-latest'

jobs:
- job: Test
  strategy:
    matrix: ${{ parameters.strategy }}
  pool:
    vmImage: ${{ matrix.imageName }}
  steps:
    - script: npm test
```

This matrix setup runs the same job across multiple operating systems concurrently, reducing total pipeline time.

Breaking Up Monolithic Pipelines

Monolithic pipelines with long-running sequential steps are prone to delays and harder to manage.

Strategies to break them up:

- Use multiple stages for different responsibilities (build, test, deploy).

- Split integration and end-to-end tests into their own pipelines or stages.

- Promote artifacts between pipelines instead of redoing work.

Benefits:

- Easier caching and troubleshooting

- Independent retries of failed stages

- Parallelization opportunities

Optimizing Docker Build Times

Docker-based builds can become slow due to layer invalidation and large image sizes.

Best Practices:

1. **Use multi-stage builds**: Separate build and runtime environments.

2. **Minimize layers**: Combine commands using && to reduce layer count.

3. **Pin base image versions**: Avoid frequent rebuilds caused by image updates.

4. **Order instructions for caching**: Place rarely changed instructions first.

```
FROM node:18-alpine AS builder
WORKDIR /app
COPY package.json ./
RUN npm install
COPY . .
RUN npm run build
```

Caching Docker Layers in Azure DevOps

Use self-hosted agents or a Docker registry to cache image layers between runs.

Reusing Pre-Built Artifacts

Rather than building everything from scratch, store and reuse:

- Build   outputs

- Compiled   binaries

- Docker   images

- Dependency   graphs

Example: Download Build Artifacts

```
- task: DownloadBuildArtifacts@0
  inputs:
    buildType: 'specific'
    project: 'MyProject'
    pipeline: 101
    buildVersionToDownload: 'latest'
    downloadPath: '$(Pipeline.Workspace)/prebuilt'
```

This retrieves previously built files for further use.

Choosing the Right Agent Pools

Azure DevOps offers:

- **Microsoft-hosted agents**: Convenient but can have cold start delays.

- **Self-hosted agents**: Persistent, customizable environments that maintain local caches.

- **Scale sets**: Auto-scale agents based on demand.

Use self-hosted agents for:

- Faster   start-up

- Larger   builds

- Persistent   toolchains   and   caches

Minimizing Step Overhead

Each task or script introduces I/O and startup overhead. Reducing unnecessary steps, combining commands, and avoiding redundant operations can shave off seconds or minutes.

Instead of:

```
- script: echo "Installing deps"
- script: npm install
```

Use:

```
- script: |
    echo "Installing deps"
    npm install
```

Reducing Logging Overhead

Verbose logging can slow down pipelines, especially in long-running loops or large builds.

Tips:

- Use `quiet` flags (`--silent`, `--quiet`) in package managers and compilers.

- Limit `echo` and debug prints unless troubleshooting.

- Redirect output to files if needed for debugging later.

Monitoring and Benchmarking

Measure the impact of optimizations by comparing:

- Pipeline duration

- Step runtimes

- Agent provisioning times

- Cache hit/miss ratios

Use tools like:

- Azure DevOps built-in analytics
- Custom telemetry with Application Insights or Log Analytics
- Third-party dashboard tools (e.g., Datadog, Grafana)

Best Practices Summary

1. **Cache everything you can**: Dependencies, build outputs, test results.

2. **Run in parallel**: Use jobs and matrix strategies to leverage concurrency.

3. **Use self-hosted agents**: For large projects with complex builds.

4. **Use fast, minimal base images**: Alpine Linux or slim Docker images.

5. **Build incrementally**: Avoid redoing work every run.

6. **Avoid redundant steps**: Combine commands and simplify logic.

7. **Tune scripts for performance**: Use async tools and minimal logging.

8. **Monitor continuously**: Pipeline speed is a long-term investment.

Conclusion

Optimizing CI build performance is a continuous effort that pays dividends in speed, cost, and developer satisfaction. By caching aggressively, leveraging parallelism, avoiding redundancy, and choosing the right infrastructure, teams can build fast, reliable pipelines in Azure DevOps that scale with their development needs.

Use data to guide your decisions, experiment with changes in isolated branches, and always benchmark your optimizations. Over time, a few seconds saved here and there can add up to hours—and dramatically improve your DevOps efficiency.

Chapter 6. Designing and Deploying CD Pipelines

Continuous Delivery vs Continuous Deployment

In the modern DevOps landscape, organizations strive to deliver software more efficiently, reliably, and frequently. Two core practices that support these goals are **Continuous Delivery** and **Continuous Deployment**. While they are often used interchangeably, they represent different levels of automation and maturity within the software delivery process. Understanding their distinctions, advantages, and implementation within Azure DevOps is key to building scalable, high-performing deployment pipelines.

What is Continuous Delivery?

Continuous Delivery (CD) is the practice of ensuring that code changes are automatically built, tested, and prepared for a release to production. In this model, every change that passes automated testing is considered deployable, but the actual deployment to production is a **manual** process, typically requiring an approval step or a decision by a release manager.

Key principles of Continuous Delivery include:

- **Automated builds and tests**: Every change triggers a pipeline that builds the code and runs tests.

- **Consistent environments**: Deployments happen to staging or UAT environments to simulate production as closely as possible.

- **Manual promotion to production**: Releases can be triggered by human intervention once validation is complete.

What is Continuous Deployment?

Continuous Deployment takes the automation one step further. In this model, every change that passes all stages of the pipeline—including automated tests—is automatically released to production. There is **no manual approval** step.

Key characteristics:

- **Fully automated pipeline** from commit to production.

- **Immediate feedback** for developers and stakeholders.

- **Higher release frequency**, often multiple times a day.

While Continuous Deployment can significantly accelerate value delivery, it requires a mature test automation strategy and high confidence in quality gates.

Comparison Table

Feature	Continuous Delivery	Continuous Deployment
Manual approval before release	Yes	No
Automated testing	Required	Required
Deployment frequency	Scheduled or manual	Immediate after pipeline
Risk level	Lower	Higher (needs solid testing)
Use case	Regulated industries, staged releases	Startups, fast-moving teams

Implementing CD Pipelines in Azure DevOps

Azure DevOps supports both Continuous Delivery and Continuous Deployment through its **Pipelines** feature. You can define a release pipeline that is triggered by successful builds and test results.

Let's walk through how to implement a basic CD pipeline with deployment to an Azure App Service.

Step 1: Prerequisites

Before creating the pipeline, ensure you have:

- An Azure DevOps project with source code in a repository.

- A successful CI pipeline that outputs a build artifact (e.g., a zipped web app).

- An Azure App Service resource created and accessible.

Step 2: Create a Release Pipeline

In Azure DevOps:

1. Navigate to **Pipelines** > **Releases**.

2. Click **New pipeline**.

3. Select **Empty job**.

4. Add a stage (e.g., "Staging" or "Production").

5. Add an **Artifact**:

   - Source type: `Build`

   - Project: Your DevOps project

   - Source (build pipeline): Your CI pipeline

   - Default version: Latest

   - Alias: `drop` (default)

6. In the stage, click **Add a task** and search for `Azure App Service deploy`.

7. Fill in the required details:

   - Azure subscription

   - App Service name

   - Package or folder: `$(System.DefaultWorkingDirectory)/drop/*.zip`

8. Save and **Create a release** to test.

YAML Alternative

Azure now supports YAML-defined pipelines for both CI and CD. Here's a sample CD configuration for deploying a Node.js app:

```
trigger:
  branches:
    include:
```

```yaml
    - main


stages:
- stage: Build
  jobs:
  - job: BuildJob
    pool:
      vmImage: 'ubuntu-latest'
    steps:
      - task: NodeTool@0
        inputs:
          versionSpec: '14.x'
      - script: |
          npm install
          npm run build
        displayName: 'Install and Build'
      - task: ArchiveFiles@2
        inputs:
          rootFolderOrFile: '$(Build.ArtifactStagingDirectory)'
          includeRootFolder: false
          archiveType: 'zip'
          archiveFile: '$(Build.ArtifactStagingDirectory)/app.zip'
      - task: PublishBuildArtifacts@1
        inputs:
```

```
            pathToPublish: '$(Build.ArtifactStagingDirectory)'

            artifactName: 'drop'


- stage: Deploy

  dependsOn: Build

  condition: succeeded()

  jobs:

  - deployment: DeployWebApp

    environment: 'production'

    strategy:

      runOnce:

        deploy:

          steps:

          - task: AzureWebApp@1

            inputs:

              azureSubscription: '<Your Connection>'

              appType: 'webApp'

              appName: '<App Service Name>'

              package: '$(Pipeline.Workspace)/drop/app.zip'
```

Step 3: Add Approvals (Continuous Delivery)

If you want to follow Continuous Delivery instead of full automation, Azure DevOps lets you add **pre-deployment approvals**.

1. Go to the environment settings (e.g., Production).

2. Under **Pre-deployment conditions**, turn on **Pre-deployment approvals**.

3. Select one or more users/groups who must approve before the release progresses.

This ensures deployments to critical environments like production are not automatic and require a human checkpoint.

Step 4: Enable Continuous Deployment Trigger

You can configure the release pipeline to be automatically triggered when a new build artifact is available.

1. In the Release pipeline, click the lightning bolt icon next to the artifact.

2. Enable the **Continuous deployment trigger**.

3. Save your changes.

Now, whenever your CI pipeline completes and produces an artifact, the CD pipeline will be triggered.

Managing Multiple Environments

Azure DevOps supports multiple environments, such as:

- **Development**

- **Staging**

- **Production**

Each can have its own deployment steps, approval gates, and rollback strategies. Use environment-specific variables and configuration files to customize behavior.

Example:

```
variables:

  devWebApp: 'myapp-dev'

  prodWebApp: 'myapp-prod'


steps:

- task: AzureWebApp@1
```

```
inputs:

  appName: '$(devWebApp)' # or $(prodWebApp) depending on stage
```

Best Practices

- **Use infrastructure as code** (e.g., ARM, Bicep, or Terraform) to ensure repeatable deployments.

- **Automate as much as possible**, but retain manual gates where risk is high.

- **Implement canary or blue-green deployments** to reduce risk in production.

- **Monitor deployments** via telemetry tools like Azure Monitor or Application Insights.

- **Ensure rollback plans** are documented and executable in case of failure.

Challenges and Considerations

- **Test coverage**: Full automation requires confidence in test suites.

- **State management**: Be cautious with stateful services and database changes.

- **Deployment velocity vs safety**: Finding the right balance between speed and control is critical.

- **Compliance**: Regulated industries may require audit trails and enforced approvals.

Summary

Choosing between Continuous Delivery and Continuous Deployment depends on your team's maturity, business needs, and risk tolerance. Azure DevOps provides flexible tools to implement either approach with robust configuration, visibility, and control. By building a well-structured CD pipeline, your organization can reduce time to market, improve quality, and respond faster to customer needs—all while maintaining governance and security.

Chapter 4: Building Your First CI Pipeline

Continuous Delivery vs Continuous Deployment

In the modern DevOps landscape, organizations strive to deliver software more efficiently, reliably, and frequently. Two core practices that support these goals are **Continuous Delivery** and **Continuous Deployment**. While they are often used interchangeably, they represent different levels of automation and maturity within the software delivery process. Understanding their distinctions, advantages, and implementation within Azure DevOps is key to building scalable, high-performing deployment pipelines.

What is Continuous Delivery?

Continuous Delivery (CD) is the practice of ensuring that code changes are automatically built, tested, and prepared for a release to production. In this model, every change that passes automated testing is considered deployable, but the actual deployment to production is a **manual** process, typically requiring an approval step or a decision by a release manager.

Key principles of Continuous Delivery include:

- **Automated builds and tests**: Every change triggers a pipeline that builds the code and runs tests.

- **Consistent environments**: Deployments happen to staging or UAT environments to simulate production as closely as possible.

- **Manual promotion to production**: Releases can be triggered by human intervention once validation is complete.

What is Continuous Deployment?

Continuous Deployment takes the automation one step further. In this model, every change that passes all stages of the pipeline—including automated tests—is automatically released to production. There is **no manual approval** step.

Key characteristics:

- **Fully automated pipeline** from commit to production.

- **Immediate feedback** for developers and stakeholders.

- **Higher release frequency**, often multiple times a day.

While Continuous Deployment can significantly accelerate value delivery, it requires a mature test automation strategy and high confidence in quality gates.

Comparison Table

Feature	Continuous Delivery	Continuous Deployment
Manual approval before release	Yes	No
Automated testing	Required	Required
Deployment frequency	Scheduled or manual	Immediate after pipeline
Risk level	Lower	Higher (needs solid testing)
Use case	Regulated industries, staged releases	Startups, fast-moving teams

Implementing CD Pipelines in Azure DevOps

Azure DevOps supports both Continuous Delivery and Continuous Deployment through its **Pipelines** feature. You can define a release pipeline that is triggered by successful builds and test results.

Let's walk through how to implement a basic CD pipeline with deployment to an Azure App Service.

Step 1: Prerequisites

Before creating the pipeline, ensure you have:

- An Azure DevOps project with source code in a repository.

- A successful CI pipeline that outputs a build artifact (e.g., a zipped web app).

- An Azure App Service resource created and accessible.

Step 2: Create a Release Pipeline

In Azure DevOps:

1. Navigate to **Pipelines** > **Releases**.

2. Click **New pipeline**.

3. Select **Empty job**.

4. Add a stage (e.g., "Staging" or "Production").

5. Add an **Artifact**:

   ○ Source type: `Build`

   ○ Project: Your DevOps project

   ○ Source (build pipeline): Your CI pipeline

   ○ Default version: Latest

   ○ Alias: `drop` (default)

6. In the stage, click **Add a task** and search for `Azure App Service deploy`.

7. Fill in the required details:

   ○ Azure subscription

   ○ App Service name

   ○ Package or folder: `$(System.DefaultWorkingDirectory)/drop/*.zip`

8. Save and **Create a release** to test.

YAML Alternative

Azure now supports YAML-defined pipelines for both CI and CD. Here's a sample CD configuration for deploying a Node.js app:

```
trigger:
  branches:
    include:
      - main
```

```yaml
stages:
- stage: Build
  jobs:
  - job: BuildJob
    pool:
      vmImage: 'ubuntu-latest'
    steps:
      - task: NodeTool@0
        inputs:
          versionSpec: '14.x'
      - script: |
          npm install
          npm run build
        displayName: 'Install and Build'
      - task: ArchiveFiles@2
        inputs:
          rootFolderOrFile: '$(Build.ArtifactStagingDirectory)'
          includeRootFolder: false
          archiveType: 'zip'
          archiveFile: '$(Build.ArtifactStagingDirectory)/app.zip'
      - task: PublishBuildArtifacts@1
        inputs:
          pathToPublish: '$(Build.ArtifactStagingDirectory)'
```

```
      artifactName: 'drop'


- stage: Deploy

  dependsOn: Build

  condition: succeeded()

  jobs:

  - deployment: DeployWebApp

    environment: 'production'

    strategy:

      runOnce:

        deploy:

          steps:

          - task: AzureWebApp@1

            inputs:

              azureSubscription: '<Your Connection>'

              appType: 'webApp'

              appName: '<App Service Name>'

              package: '$(Pipeline.Workspace)/drop/app.zip'
```

Step 3: Add Approvals (Continuous Delivery)

If you want to follow Continuous Delivery instead of full automation, Azure DevOps lets you add **pre-deployment approvals**.

1. Go to the environment settings (e.g., Production).

2. Under **Pre-deployment conditions**, turn on **Pre-deployment approvals**.

3. Select one or more users/groups who must approve before the release progresses.

This ensures deployments to critical environments like production are not automatic and require a human checkpoint.

Step 4: Enable Continuous Deployment Trigger

You can configure the release pipeline to be automatically triggered when a new build artifact is available.

1. In the Release pipeline, click the lightning bolt icon next to the artifact.

2. Enable the **Continuous deployment trigger**.

3. Save your changes.

Now, whenever your CI pipeline completes and produces an artifact, the CD pipeline will be triggered.

Managing Multiple Environments

Azure DevOps supports multiple environments, such as:

- **Development**

- **Staging**

- **Production**

Each can have its own deployment steps, approval gates, and rollback strategies. Use environment-specific variables and configuration files to customize behavior.

Example:

```
variables:

  devWebApp: 'myapp-dev'

  prodWebApp: 'myapp-prod'


steps:

- task: AzureWebApp@1

  inputs:

    appName: '$(devWebApp)' # or $(prodWebApp) depending on stage
```

Best Practices

- **Use infrastructure as code** (e.g., ARM, Bicep, or Terraform) to ensure repeatable deployments.

- **Automate as much as possible**, but retain manual gates where risk is high.

- **Implement canary or blue-green deployments** to reduce risk in production.

- **Monitor deployments** via telemetry tools like Azure Monitor or Application Insights.

- **Ensure rollback plans** are documented and executable in case of failure.

Challenges and Considerations

- **Test coverage**: Full automation requires confidence in test suites.

- **State management**: Be cautious with stateful services and database changes.

- **Deployment velocity vs safety**: Finding the right balance between speed and control is critical.

- **Compliance**: Regulated industries may require audit trails and enforced approvals.

Summary

Choosing between Continuous Delivery and Continuous Deployment depends on your team's maturity, business needs, and risk tolerance. Azure DevOps provides flexible tools to implement either approach with robust configuration, visibility, and control. By building a well-structured CD pipeline, your organization can reduce time to market, improve quality, and respond faster to customer needs—all while maintaining governance and security.

Creating Release Pipelines

Creating release pipelines in Azure DevOps is a fundamental step in implementing a robust Continuous Delivery (CD) strategy. These pipelines are responsible for taking validated artifacts from the CI process and deploying them to various environments like development, staging, and production. A release pipeline orchestrates the deployment workflow, incorporates approvals and gates, and ensures smooth transitions between stages. This section provides a detailed, hands-on guide to creating and managing release pipelines in Azure DevOps, encompassing both classic UI-based pipelines and YAML-based deployments.

Understanding Release Pipelines

A release pipeline is composed of:

- **Artifacts**: The output from a CI build (e.g., compiled code, packaged application).

- **Stages**: Logical groupings representing environments such as Dev, Test, and Prod.

- **Jobs and Tasks**: Units of execution that perform deployment or validation.

- **Approvals and Gates**: Mechanisms for enforcing policies and ensuring quality before progressing.

Release pipelines help enforce **repeatability, traceability, and governance,** making them essential for enterprise-grade deployments.

Creating a Release Pipeline Using the Azure DevOps Classic Editor

Step 1: Navigate to Releases

1. In Azure DevOps, go to **Pipelines > Releases.**

2. Click **New pipeline.**

3. Choose **Start with an empty job** or select a template based on your use case (e.g., App Service deployment).

Step 2: Add an Artifact

1. Click **Add an artifact.**

2. Choose **Build** as the source type.

3. Select the project and the relevant build pipeline.

4. Use the latest version of the artifact and give it an alias (commonly drop).

5. Save your progress.

Step 3: Define Stages

Stages represent deployment targets. A pipeline can have a single stage or multiple sequential stages (Dev → Staging → Prod).

1. Rename the default stage (e.g., "Dev Deployment").

2. Click on the stage to add tasks.

3. Choose tasks like:

   o Azure App Service Deploy

   o Azure CLI

   o ARM Template Deployment

   o PowerShell Script

Example deployment task configuration:

- **App Service name**: my-app-dev

- **Package or folder**: $(System.DefaultWorkingDirectory)/drop/*.zip

- **App type**: Web App on Windows

Step 4: Clone Stages for Other Environments

Once a Dev stage is configured, you can clone it for other environments like Staging or Production:

1. Click the **clone** button on the Dev stage.

2. Rename to "Staging Deployment."

3. Change variables and tasks specific to the environment.

Step 5: Add Approvals and Gates

1. Click the **Pre-deployment conditions** icon (person with checkmark).

2. Turn on **Pre-deployment approvals**.

3. Add required approvers (e.g., QA manager, Product owner).

4. Optionally, configure **gates**:

   o Query Azure Monitor alerts

        ○   Invoke   REST   APIs

        ○   Check   work   item   queries

Approvals ensure human oversight in sensitive environments like production.

Step 6: Configure Continuous Deployment Trigger

1. Click the lightning bolt icon on the artifact.

2. Enable **Continuous deployment trigger**.

3. This ensures a new release is automatically created when a new build is available.

Step 7: Save and Create a Release

1. Click **Save** and name the pipeline.

2. Click **Create release**.

3. Choose the stages to deploy to and proceed.

Creating Release Pipelines with YAML

While classic pipelines are intuitive, YAML pipelines offer better flexibility, versioning, and code-as-infrastructure capabilities.

Below is an example of a multi-stage YAML pipeline that handles both build and deployment to Azure App Service:

```yaml
trigger:
  branches:
    include:
      - main

stages:
- stage: Build
  jobs:
```

```yaml
  - job: BuildJob
    pool:
      vmImage: 'ubuntu-latest'
    steps:
      - task: NodeTool@0
        inputs:
          versionSpec: '16.x'
      - script: |
          npm install
          npm run build
        displayName: 'Build Application'
      - task: PublishBuildArtifacts@1
        inputs:
          pathToPublish: '$(Build.ArtifactStagingDirectory)'
          artifactName: 'drop'

- stage: DeployDev
  dependsOn: Build
  jobs:
    - deployment: DeployDev
      environment: 'dev'
      strategy:
        runOnce:
          deploy:
```

```
          steps:

            - task: AzureWebApp@1

              inputs:

                azureSubscription: '<Azure Connection>'

                appName: 'myapp-dev'

                package: '$(Pipeline.Workspace)/drop/*.zip'


- stage: DeployProd

  dependsOn: DeployDev

  condition: succeeded()

  jobs:

    - deployment: DeployProd

      environment: 'production'

      strategy:

        runOnce:

          deploy:

            steps:

              - task: AzureWebApp@1

                inputs:

                  azureSubscription: '<Azure Connection>'

                  appName: 'myapp-prod'

                  package: '$(Pipeline.Workspace)/drop/*.zip'
```

Key Features of YAML Pipelines

- **Version control**: Pipeline definition resides in source code.

- **Reusable templates**: Define standard deployment logic once and reuse.

- **Environment-specific configuration**: Use variable groups or parameter files.

Managing Secrets with Azure Key Vault

When working with pipelines, sensitive information (e.g., API keys, passwords) should not be hardcoded. Azure DevOps integrates seamlessly with **Azure Key Vault**.

To use Key Vault secrets:

1. Create a Key Vault and add secrets.

2. In Azure DevOps, link the Key Vault to a variable group.

3. Reference secrets in tasks:

```
variables:
  - group: KeyVaultSecrets


steps:
  - script: echo $(mySecret)
```

This keeps secrets out of code and pipelines.

Deployment Strategies

Azure DevOps supports several deployment strategies:

- **Canary deployments**: Gradually roll out to users.

- **Blue-green deployments**: Maintain two identical environments; switch traffic.

- **Rolling deployments**: Update portions of infrastructure incrementally.

Each strategy can be configured via custom logic in YAML pipelines or using task extensions and Azure Traffic Manager.

Monitoring and Auditing Releases

Azure DevOps provides extensive logging and auditing:

- **Pipeline logs**: Per-task logs for each deployment.

- **Audit trails**: Track who approved or modified pipelines.

- **Telemetry**: Integrate with Application Insights or Azure Monitor for real-time monitoring.

Use alerts to notify stakeholders on deployment status, failures, or approvals.

Best Practices

- **Use variable groups** to manage environment-specific values centrally.

- **Leverage pipeline caching** for dependencies to speed up builds.

- **Include rollback mechanisms** in case deployments fail.

- **Tag releases** for traceability and auditing.

- **Segment permissions**: Not every user needs production access.

Summary

Creating release pipelines in Azure DevOps is a vital aspect of modern software delivery. Whether you opt for the visual designer or YAML pipelines, Azure DevOps offers a rich set of tools to manage artifacts, environments, and deployments. By incorporating approvals, secrets management, and environment-specific stages, you can build highly reliable and secure deployment workflows. This foundational skill paves the way for implementing robust Continuous Delivery strategies that align with business goals, regulatory requirements, and operational excellence.

Deploying to Azure App Services, VMs, and Kubernetes

Deploying applications efficiently to target environments is a core capability of any CI/CD pipeline. Azure DevOps enables streamlined, automated deployments to a variety of platforms including Azure App Services, Virtual Machines (VMs), and Kubernetes clusters. Each of these platforms has its own strengths, requirements, and best practices. This section explores in depth how to configure Azure DevOps pipelines for deploying to these environments, covering the setup, configuration, deployment process, and environment-specific considerations.

Deploying to Azure App Services

Azure App Service is a fully managed platform for hosting web applications, REST APIs, and mobile backends. It supports multiple languages including .NET, Java, PHP, Node.js, Python, and Ruby.

Key Benefits

- Managed scaling and patching

- Integrated authentication and authorization

- Built-in CI/CD support

- Easy integration with Azure DevOps

Prerequisites

- An Azure subscription

- An App Service plan and App Service instance created

- A build pipeline that produces an artifact (e.g., a zipped web app)

Setting Up Deployment

You can use the **Azure App Service Deploy** task in classic pipelines or define your deployment with YAML.

Classic Pipeline Task

1. In the release pipeline, add the `Azure App Service deploy` task.

2. Choose the subscription and authorize.

3. Select the App type (e.g., Web App on Windows).

4. Select the App Service name.

5. Set the package or folder path, typically:

```
$(System.DefaultWorkingDirectory)/drop/*.zip
```

6. Save   and   deploy.

YAML Example

```
- task: AzureWebApp@1

  inputs:

    azureSubscription: 'MyAzureSubscription'

    appName: 'my-app-service-name'

    package: '$(Pipeline.Workspace)/drop/app.zip'
```

Configuration Tips

- Use deployment slots (e.g., staging, production) for zero-downtime deployments.

- Configure app settings and connection strings in Azure Portal or through the Azure CLI.

- Enable   Application   Insights   for   monitoring.

Deploying to Azure Virtual Machines (VMs)

For applications requiring full control of the OS or legacy environments, Azure VMs provide a flexible solution. You can deploy to VMs via:

- Azure   DevOps   agent   installed   on   the   VM

- SSH   (Linux)   or   WinRM   (Windows)

- Azure   DevOps   Deployment   Groups

Option 1: Deployment Groups

1. In   Azure   DevOps,   go   to   **Pipelines   >   Deployment   groups**.

2. Create   a   new   deployment   group   (e.g.,   WebVMGroup).

3. Copy the script and run it on the target VM as Administrator (Windows) or sudo (Linux).

4. Once the VM is registered, it will appear in the group.

Adding to Pipeline

1. In the release pipeline, add a **Deployment Group job**.

2. Select your deployment group.

3. Add tasks such as:

   o Copy Files

   o Azure File Copy

   o PowerShell or Bash

Example:

```
jobs:

- deployment: DeployToVM

  environment:

    name: 'WebVMGroup'

    resourceType: VirtualMachine

  strategy:

    runOnce:

      deploy:

        steps:

          - task: CopyFiles@2

            inputs:

              SourceFolder: '$(Pipeline.Workspace)/drop'

              Contents: '**'

              TargetFolder: 'C:\inetpub\wwwroot'
```

```
- task: PowerShell@2

  inputs:

    targetType: inline

    script: |

      Restart-Service -Name 'w3svc'
```

Option 2: SSH Deployment (Linux)

You can also deploy directly using SSH if no agent is installed.

```
- task: CopyFilesOverSSH@0

  inputs:

    sshEndpoint: 'LinuxVMConnection'

    sourceFolder: '$(Pipeline.Workspace)/drop'

    targetFolder: '/var/www/myapp'
```

Best Practices

- Automate firewall rules and VM provisioning with Terraform or ARM templates.

- Store credentials securely using service connections and secrets.

- Configure auto-restart for critical services after deployment.

Deploying to Azure Kubernetes Service (AKS)

Azure Kubernetes Service (AKS) offers a managed Kubernetes platform that simplifies deploying, managing, and scaling containerized applications using Kubernetes.

Prerequisites

- An AKS cluster deployed and accessible

- A container image built and stored in a container registry (e.g., ACR or Docker Hub)

- A Helm chart or Kubernetes manifests

Connecting Azure DevOps to AKS

1. Create a service connection in Azure DevOps for your AKS cluster using Azure Resource Manager.

2. Ensure the pipeline agent has access to `kubectl` and `helm` (use Microsoft-hosted agents).

Sample YAML Pipeline

```
trigger:

  branches:

    include:

      - main



stages:

- stage: BuildAndPush

  jobs:

    - job: Build

      pool:

        vmImage: 'ubuntu-latest'

      steps:

        - task: Docker@2

          inputs:

            containerRegistry: 'MyACR'

            repository: 'myapp'
```

```
            command: 'buildAndPush'

            Dockerfile: '**/Dockerfile'

            tags: latest


- stage: DeployToAKS

  dependsOn: BuildAndPush

  jobs:

    - deployment: Deploy

      environment: 'aks-cluster.default'

      strategy:

        runOnce:

          deploy:

            steps:

              - task: HelmInstaller@1

                inputs:

                  helmVersionToInstall: 'latest'

              - task: HelmDeploy@0

                inputs:

                  connectionType: 'Azure Resource Manager'

                  azureSubscription: 'MyAzureSubscription'

                  azureResourceGroup: 'my-rg'

                  kubernetesCluster: 'my-aks-cluster'

                  command: 'upgrade'

                  chartType: 'FilePath'
```

```
        chartPath: 'charts/myapp'

        releaseName: 'myapp'

        overrideValues: |

            image.repository=myregistry.azurecr.io/myapp

            image.tag=latest
```

Kubernetes Manifests

You can also deploy using raw Kubernetes YAML:

```
- task: KubernetesManifest@0

  inputs:

    action: deploy

    kubernetesServiceConnection: 'MyAKSConnection'

    manifests: |

      manifests/deployment.yaml

      manifests/service.yaml

    containers: |

      myregistry.azurecr.io/myapp:latest
```

Managing Multi-Environment Deployments

When deploying to multiple environments (e.g., dev, test, prod), it's important to:

- Parameterize   configurations

- Use   Helm   values   files   or   Kubernetes   ConfigMaps

- Leverage Azure DevOps **environments** for visualization, auditing, and approvals

Example Helm value override:

```
--set environment=staging \
--set replicaCount=2 \
--set image.tag=latest
```

Security Considerations

- Use managed identities or service principals for secure resource access.

- Avoid storing secrets in pipeline YAML—use Azure Key Vault integration.

- Restrict access to production environments with approvals and RBAC.

Monitoring Deployments

- Integrate with **Azure Monitor**, **Log Analytics**, or **Prometheus** for observability.

- Use probes (`liveness`, `readiness`) in Kubernetes for self-healing deployments.

- Configure alerts on metrics like error rate, response time, and CPU usage.

Troubleshooting Common Issues

Platform	Issue	Solution
App Service	"404 after deployment"	Check deployment path and app offline file
VMs	File not found	Verify file copy task and permissions
Kubernetes	CrashLoopBackOff in pods	Check logs with `kubectl logs`, verify image and configs

| All | Authentication failures | Review service connections and permissions |

Summary

Deploying to Azure App Services, VMs, and Kubernetes using Azure DevOps allows for flexible, scalable, and consistent release strategies tailored to different application architectures and operational requirements. App Services suit web apps with minimal infrastructure management. VMs support custom OS configurations and legacy apps. Kubernetes empowers containerized microservices with high scalability and resilience. By leveraging Azure DevOps' pipeline capabilities, organizations can automate deployments to any of these platforms, ensuring fast, reliable, and repeatable software delivery.

Managing Environments and Approvals

Managing environments and approvals is a critical component of a robust Continuous Delivery (CD) or Continuous Deployment (CD) pipeline in Azure DevOps. This management ensures that deployments are not only automated but also secure, auditable, and compliant with organizational policies. In this section, we'll explore how to effectively structure and manage deployment environments, implement approval gates, enforce governance, and leverage environment-specific configurations and auditing features.

Understanding Environments in Azure DevOps

An **environment** in Azure DevOps represents a logical grouping of resources that you deploy to, such as development, staging, and production. Environments provide a layer of abstraction over your infrastructure and allow for enhanced tracking, approvals, and visualization.

Key Benefits

- **Auditable** **deployments** across environments

- **Traceability** of changes, approvers, and deployment history

- **Approval** **gates** for secure release promotion

- **Environment-specific** **configurations** like secrets or variables

- **Resource** **views** for infrastructure like Kubernetes or VMs

Creating and Using Environments

Step 1: Create an Environment

1. Navigate to **Pipelines > Environments** in Azure DevOps.

2. Click **New Environment**.

3. Provide a name (e.g., Staging, Production).

4. (Optional) Link the environment to Kubernetes, virtual machines, or another deployment target.

Step 2: Add Environment to YAML Pipeline

Environments can be defined directly within a pipeline to associate deployments with approvals, checks, and monitoring.

```
jobs:

- deployment: DeployToStaging

  environment: 'Staging'

  strategy:

    runOnce:

      deploy:

        steps:

          - script: echo Deploying to staging
```

This configuration automatically logs deployments to the "Staging" environment and allows for additional approval gates to be enforced.

Implementing Approval Gates

Azure DevOps allows you to require **manual or automated approvals** before a deployment can proceed to an environment.

Types of Gates

1. **Pre-deployment Approvals** – Required before a deployment can begin.

2. **Post-deployment Approvals** – Required after the deployment has completed.

Configuring Manual Approvals

1. Go to the environment settings in the Azure DevOps portal.

2. Under **Checks**, click **Add** and choose **Approvals and checks**.

3. Add users or groups required to approve deployments.

4. Set timeout duration, request expiration, and notifications.

```
environment:

  name: 'Production'

  resourceType: VirtualMachine

  checks:

    - approvers:

        - id: user@domain.com

        - id: devlead@company.com

      timeout: 2h
```

This adds a mandatory manual review step before any deployment proceeds to production.

Automating Checks and Governance

In addition to manual approvals, Azure DevOps allows automated **checks** before deployment:

- **Azure Monitor alerts**: Block deployments if active alerts are detected.

- **Query work items**: Require certain work item states before release (e.g., all bugs resolved).

- **Invoke REST API**: Call external services for validation (e.g., risk score or policy engine).

- **Business Hours**: Restrict deployments to approved windows.

Example: Enforcing deployments only between 9AM–5PM weekdays:

```
checks:
  - type: schedule
    schedule:
      days:
        - Monday
        - Tuesday
        - Wednesday
        - Thursday
        - Friday
      startTime: '09:00'
      endTime: '17:00'
```

Managing Environment-Specific Variables and Secrets

Different environments often require different configurations. Azure DevOps supports **variable groups** and **pipeline variables**, which can be scoped per environment.

Example: Defining Environment Variables

```
variables:
  - group: CommonSettings

jobs:
```

```
- deployment: DeployToProd

  environment: 'Production'

  strategy:

    runOnce:

      deploy:

        steps:

          - script: echo "Using connection string $(DBConnectionString)"
```

You can define environment-specific variables in variable groups or directly inside the pipeline for fine-tuned control.

Using Azure Key Vault

Securely manage secrets with Azure Key Vault:

1. Create a Key Vault and add secrets.

2. Link the vault in Azure DevOps Library > Variable Groups.

3. Enable "Link secrets from an Azure Key Vault as variables".

Then use secrets like normal variables:

```
variables:

  - group: ProductionSecrets


steps:

  - script: echo $(MySecureApiKey)
```

Visualizing Deployments

Azure DevOps provides a deployment **timeline and audit log** per environment:

- Who initiated the deployment
- When it was approved and by whom
- What version was deployed
- Status and logs for each stage

This traceability is essential for regulated industries and post-incident reviews.

Environment Strategy: Staging vs Production

A typical environment hierarchy may include:

- **Development**: Frequent, automated deployments; minimal approvals
- **Testing/Staging**: Deploy after CI passes; automated tests and approvals
- **Production**: Strict access, manual approvals, restricted hours

Example Pipeline Structure

```
stages:
- stage: DeployDev
  jobs:
    - deployment: DeployDev
      environment: 'Development'
      strategy:
        runOnce:
          deploy:
            steps:
              - script: echo "Deploying to Dev"
```

```
- stage: DeployStaging

  dependsOn: DeployDev

  jobs:

    - deployment: DeployStaging

      environment: 'Staging'

      strategy:

        runOnce:

          deploy:

            steps:

              - script: echo "Deploying to Staging"


- stage: DeployProd

  dependsOn: DeployStaging

  jobs:

    - deployment: DeployProd

      environment: 'Production'

      strategy:

        runOnce:

          deploy:

            steps:

              - script: echo "Deploying to Production"
```

Each environment can have its own approval and check configurations without duplicating the core deployment logic.

Enforcing Compliance and Governance

Using environment management and approvals, DevOps teams can:

- Enforce separation of duties (e.g., devs can't deploy to prod without approval)

- Ensure change control processes are followed

- Maintain audit trails for regulatory compliance

- Implement layered security through RBAC and policy checks

Best Practices

- **Use clearly named environments** matching their purpose (Dev, QA, Prod)

- **Automate where possible,** but enforce approvals for production

- **Use variables and templates** for consistency and reuse

- **Review environment configurations** regularly for permissions and access

- **Document your process** for internal audits and training

Summary

Effective management of environments and approvals in Azure DevOps forms the backbone of secure, auditable, and scalable deployment practices. By defining structured environments, implementing approval workflows, automating checks, and leveraging environment-specific configurations, organizations can balance the need for speed with the demands of governance. These practices not only improve confidence in releases but also help teams align with enterprise IT standards and compliance frameworks, creating a foundation for high-performing DevOps.

Chapter 7: Security, Compliance, and Best Practices

Secrets Management and Secure Pipelines

In any modern CI/CD pipeline, especially when working within enterprise environments or deploying to production systems, the security of sensitive data is paramount. Secrets such as API keys, connection strings, passwords, tokens, certificates, and other credentials must be carefully managed to avoid data breaches or unauthorized access.

Secure pipeline practices and robust secrets management processes form the backbone of a trustworthy DevOps lifecycle. Azure DevOps provides several tools and integrations to help safeguard secrets and implement best practices for secure pipelines.

Understanding the Risks of Poor Secrets Management

Before diving into tools and configurations, it's important to understand the potential risks:

- **Hardcoding secrets** in source code repositories can expose them to anyone with repository access and may lead to serious breaches.

- **Environment variable leaks** during pipeline logs or misconfigured jobs can inadvertently expose secrets to team members or the public.

- **Insecure access controls** on libraries, variable groups, or pipelines can result in privilege escalation or lateral movement attacks.

- **Lack of auditing** means there's no visibility into who accessed or changed sensitive data.

Azure DevOps Secure Options for Secrets

Azure DevOps offers several mechanisms to protect secrets:

1. Secure Pipeline Variables

Azure DevOps lets you define variables at multiple levels — pipeline-level, stage-level, or job-level. Marking a variable as a "secret" masks its value in the logs and restricts it from being printed during the job execution.

Example:

```
variables:
  - name: mySecret
```

```
value: $(MY_SECRET)

isSecret: true
```

You can also set secrets through the Azure DevOps portal when defining pipeline variables or through variable groups.

2. Variable Groups with Key Vault Integration

For better security, especially at scale, it's recommended to use **Azure Key Vault**. Azure DevOps integrates natively with Key Vault, enabling your pipelines to retrieve secrets at runtime.

To use Key Vault:

1. Create a Key Vault in your Azure subscription.

2. Add secrets (e.g., `db-connection`, `storage-access-key`).

3. Assign Azure DevOps the right permissions using a service principal or managed identity.

4. Link the Key Vault to a Variable Group in Azure DevOps.

Example:

```
variables:

- group: KeyVaultSecrets
```

Make sure the variable group is linked to a Key Vault and the secrets are mapped properly.

3. Environment Variables in Runtime Environments

When deploying to services like App Service, Kubernetes, or VMs, use environment variables to inject secrets instead of including them in application code or configuration files.

Use deployment pipeline tasks that set these securely, ensuring they're passed in at runtime.

Example (App Service Deployment):

```
- task: AzureRmWebAppDeployment@4

  inputs:
```

```
appSettings: '-MY_SECRET $(mySecret)'
```

This ensures your application gets the necessary config without exposing them in logs or files.

Protecting Secrets During Pipeline Execution

Even if secrets are stored securely, they can still be compromised if not handled correctly during pipeline execution.

Masking Secrets in Logs

Secrets passed as variables should be automatically masked by Azure DevOps in logs. Ensure logging steps avoid printing variable values directly.

Avoid:

```
- script: echo $(mySecret)
```

Instead:

Use them internally in scripts without echoing, or mask them if necessary:

```
- script: |
    export SECRET=$(mySecret)
    ./run-deployment.sh
```

If custom tooling is used that prints environment variables, make sure to audit and redact sensitive content.

Secure Agent Pools and Self-Hosted Runners

Ensure agents (especially self-hosted) are secure:

- Regularly update and patch runners.
- Use a restricted, isolated environment for running builds.
- Avoid giving agents access to excessive resources or permissions.

- Ensure that secrets aren't written to disk.

Scoped Access and Least Privilege

Always apply the principle of **least privilege**:

- Scope service connections and variable groups only to the projects that need them.

- Use RBAC (Role-Based Access Control) to control who can edit pipelines, variables, or release definitions.

- Avoid giving broad permissions unless necessary.

Key Vault Integration – End-to-End Setup

Let's walk through a secure end-to-end setup with Azure Key Vault integration in an Azure DevOps pipeline.

Step 1: Create and Configure Key Vault

```
az keyvault create --name MySecureVault --resource-group
DevOpsResources --location eastus

az keyvault secret set --vault-name MySecureVault --name "StorageKey"
--value "supersecure123"
```

Step 2: Assign Azure DevOps Service Principal Access

If you're using a service connection with a service principal:

```
az keyvault set-policy --name MySecureVault --spn <client-id> --
secret-permissions get list
```

Step 3: Create a Variable Group in Azure DevOps

- Navigate to Pipelines → Library

- Create a new Variable Group, link it to the Key Vault, and select the secrets you want to use.

- Name the group, for example, KeyVaultSecrets

Step 4: Use in YAML Pipeline

```yaml
variables:
- group: KeyVaultSecrets


jobs:
- job: SecureJob

  steps:

  - script: |

      echo "Starting deployment..."

      ./deploy.sh $(StorageKey)
```

This ensures the secret is never stored in your repo or shown in logs.

Implementing Pipeline Access Controls

Another aspect of secure pipelines is **access control**:

- **Limit who can edit pipelines**: This prevents unauthorized users from adding malicious steps.

- **Approve deployments**: Require manual approvals for production releases.

- **Use environment protection rules**: Azure DevOps environments allow for required checks before deployment.

Example:

```yaml
environments:

  - name: 'production'

    protectionRules:
```

```
    - reviewers:

      - name: 'frahaan@company.com'
```

This requires manual approval from a specified user before proceeding.

Secure Repository Practices

Security also starts with your code and repo:

- Enable **branch protection rules**.
- Require **code reviews** for all pull requests.
- Enforce **status checks** before merging.
- Scan dependencies for vulnerabilities (using tools like WhiteSource or SonarCloud).
- Rotate credentials and secrets regularly.

Auditing and Logging Secret Usage

To maintain a secure and compliant pipeline environment:

- Enable **audit logs** in Azure DevOps for sensitive operations.
- Track access to variable groups, service connections, and pipeline edits.
- Review logs periodically, especially for high-privilege users.

For example, Azure DevOps Audit Logs include:

- Secret changes
- Variable group updates
- Service connection usage
- Pipeline executions

Additional Tools and Best Practices

1. **Azure Managed Identity**: Avoid using credentials at all — use managed identities for resources like VMs or web apps to access Azure services securely.

2. **Credential Scanners**: Integrate tools like Microsoft's **CredScan**, **GitGuardian**, or **TruffleHog** into your pipeline to detect accidental leaks.

3. **Rotate and Expire Secrets**: Implement policies for periodic rotation and automated expiration of secrets.

4. **Zero Trust Practices**: Don't trust any network segment or user by default. Always verify before granting access.

5. **Policy as Code**: Use tools like **OPA (Open Policy Agent)** or **Azure Policy** to enforce security rules at infrastructure and code level.

Summary

Secrets management is not just a technical implementation—it's a discipline that requires continuous vigilance, governance, and automation. Azure DevOps provides a strong framework for securing your pipelines, especially when used with services like Azure Key Vault and role-based access controls.

To secure your pipelines:

- Never hardcode secrets.
- Use secret variables and Key Vault.
- Secure your agents.
- Audit and review access regularly.
- Automate secret rotation and integrate scanners.

By building a culture of secure development and deployment, teams can move fast without compromising safety.

Policy Enforcement and Auditing

As organizations scale their DevOps practices, it becomes crucial to ensure consistent enforcement of policies and robust auditing across the CI/CD pipeline. This helps maintain compliance, reduce risk, and ensure the integrity of software delivery processes.

In Azure DevOps, policy enforcement refers to implementing governance controls over code repositories, pipelines, environments, and release processes. Auditing, on the other hand, is about maintaining visibility into changes, tracking actions, and detecting anomalies. Together, these practices form the backbone of secure and compliant DevOps operations.

Importance of Policy Enforcement

Policy enforcement ensures that teams do not bypass critical processes such as code reviews, testing, and approvals. Key reasons for implementing strong policy enforcement include:

- **Maintaining regulatory compliance** (e.g., SOC 2, ISO 27001, HIPAA)

- **Reducing human error** in deployments and configuration

- **Preventing unauthorized changes** to source code or production environments

- **Automating guardrails** that allow teams to move fast without breaking rules

Types of Policies in Azure DevOps

Azure DevOps supports policy enforcement in several areas:

1. Branch Policies

Branch policies in Azure Repos are the first line of defense against unwanted or risky code entering your main branch.

Key policies include:

- **Require a minimum number of reviewers** before merging a pull request

- **Check for linked work items** to enforce traceability

- **Require successful build completion** to ensure code quality

- **Limit who can push directly** to protected branches

Example configuration via Azure DevOps portal:

- Protect `main` branch

- Require 2 code reviewers

- Enforce successful pipeline run `(CI-Validation)`

- Block force pushes

YAML-based enforcement isn't supported natively for branch policies, but you can script configuration using the Azure DevOps REST API.

2. Pipeline Policies

Pipeline governance ensures CI/CD processes adhere to standards. Key aspects include:

- **Mandatory pipeline approvals** before running deployments

- **Pipeline locking** to restrict who can edit or trigger builds

- **Environment checks and gates** before promoting artifacts

- **Timeouts and limits** on job execution to prevent abuse

For example, to require approval for production:

```
environments:

  - name: 'Production'

    protectionRules:

      - reviewers:

          - name: 'ops-team@company.com'
```

3. Environment Protection Rules

These control deployments to environments such as staging or production.

Rules include:

- **Manual** approvals

- **Azure** Function gates

- **Invoke** REST API gates

- **Business** **hours** **deployment** **restrictions**
- **Exclusion** **of** **weekends** **or** **holidays**

These can be set via the Azure DevOps UI or using the `az pipelines` CLI.

4. Resource Authorization

Azure DevOps lets you restrict pipelines from accessing specific resources unless explicitly authorized.

For example:

- Variable groups
- Service connections
- Secure files
- Environments

Only authorized pipelines can consume these, protecting sensitive infrastructure or secrets.

Auditing in Azure DevOps

While policy enforcement restricts unwanted behavior, auditing tracks what actually happens. It allows teams to detect unauthorized access, understand incident causes, and comply with regulations.

1. Audit Logs

Azure DevOps provides audit logs to track activity at the organization level.

You can monitor:

- Pipeline edits and runs
- Permission changes
- Project-level settings changes
- User account activity
- Variable or secret updates

- Service connection configuration changes

These logs can be exported via:

- **Azure DevOps UI**
- **REST API**
- **Azure Monitor or Sentinel** for advanced analytics

To access logs:

- Go to Organization Settings → Auditing
- Filter by event type, user, or date range
- Download for offline review

2. Pipeline Logging and Traceability

Each pipeline run contains detailed logs for every step. Best practices include:

- Logging all deployment actions (excluding secrets)
- Adding trace IDs for cross-system correlation
- Retaining logs based on compliance retention policies (e.g., 90 or 180 days)

Azure DevOps allows retention policy settings per pipeline or globally.

```
trigger:

- main


pool:

  vmImage: 'ubuntu-latest'


jobs:

- job: auditExample
```

```
steps:

- script: |

    echo       "Deploying      version      $(Build.BuildId)      by
$(Build.RequestedFor)"
```

Ensure sensitive data is excluded or masked, and avoid excessive logging of internal configurations.

Enforcing Policy as Code

Policy enforcement can be treated as code by using external tools or Azure-native integrations.

Using Azure Policy

Azure Policy lets you define and enforce rules at the subscription level, such as:

- Only approved Azure regions can be used
- Tags like environment=production must be applied
- Storage accounts must use encryption

These policies can be applied to resources deployed via ARM templates, Bicep, or Terraform.

Using GitHub and Rego (OPA)

If your code is stored in GitHub and synced with Azure DevOps, policy-as-code can be enforced using GitHub Actions and **Open Policy Agent (OPA)**.

Example OPA policy:

```
package ci.policy


deny[msg] {

  input.pipeline.environment == "prod"

  not input.approved_by_admin
```

```
  msg := "Production deployments require admin approval"

}
```

OPA can run in CI to block merges or deployments based on policy violations.

Implementing Approval Workflows

Manual or automated approvals can be embedded into pipelines to ensure human review or external system checks before proceeding.

Manual Approval Gates

Azure DevOps allows defining pre-deployment approvals. Reviewers must approve within a timeout window (e.g., 48 hours), or deployment is blocked.

```
environments:

- name: 'Production'

  checks:

  - type: 'Approval'

    reviewers:

      - id: 'frahaan@company.com'
```

Automated Approval Gates

Use external REST APIs or Azure Functions to programmatically allow or block deployments. These can check external systems, compliance scores, or run integration tests.

```
environments:

  - name: 'Staging'

    checks:

      - type: invokeRESTAPI

        url: https://check-my-policy.com/validate
```

```
method: POST
```

Enforcing Build and Release Standards

Set organization-wide standards for:

- **Naming conventions** for pipelines and environments
- **Tagging builds** with version or change references
- **Enforcing artifact retention policies**
- **Using templates for consistent pipeline definitions**

Templates help enforce logic reuse and consistent practices:

```
# template: build-template.yml

parameters:

  - name: language

    type: string


steps:

  - script: echo "Running build for ${{ parameters.language }}"
```

Then used in pipelines:

```
extends:

  template: build-template.yml

  parameters:

    language: 'dotnet'
```

This approach ensures that builds follow common patterns, reducing mistakes and increasing maintainability.

Compliance Considerations

For regulated industries, Azure DevOps provides several features to support compliance:

- **Audit logs and export**
- **Secure variables and secrets**
- **Manual and automated approval gates**
- **Environment-level controls**
- **Support for DevOps process documentation**

Consider integrating Azure DevOps with tools like:

- **Azure Monitor** or **Log Analytics** for log centralization
- **Microsoft Sentinel** for threat detection
- **Compliance Manager** for assessing standards like GDPR, ISO 27001, NIST, etc.

Always document your CI/CD controls and review them regularly to meet audit requirements.

Summary

Policy enforcement and auditing in Azure DevOps are critical for building secure, resilient, and compliant CI/CD pipelines. By implementing strong guardrails and maintaining detailed logs, organizations can:

- Prevent unauthorized changes
- Detect and respond to incidents quickly
- Prove compliance during audits
- Standardize software delivery across teams

Best practices include:

- Using branch and pipeline policies

- Protecting environments with approval workflows

- Leveraging Azure Key Vault and access controls

- Treating policies as code

- Continuously auditing actions and logs

By treating governance as a first-class concern in your DevOps lifecycle, you empower teams to deliver fast while staying safe and compliant.

Compliance Standards and CI/CD Governance

Modern software development does not operate in a vacuum—it must comply with regulatory, legal, and industry-specific standards. In the context of CI/CD, compliance standards ensure that the continuous integration and deployment pipelines meet rigorous requirements for security, privacy, availability, and traceability. Azure DevOps provides the tools, features, and integrations necessary to build governance directly into your DevOps processes.

Governance is not about slowing down development—it's about enabling responsible innovation. When designed well, governance frameworks can help teams move faster by reducing risk, ensuring clarity, and automating compliance.

Understanding Compliance in CI/CD

Compliance standards vary by industry and region, but they typically include requirements such as:

- **Data privacy** and user consent (e.g., GDPR, HIPAA)

- **Auditability** of system changes and user actions

- **Security controls** over code, infrastructure, and credentials

- **Change management** and approvals

- **Availability and disaster recovery**

- **Configuration consistency** and infrastructure as code

Key compliance frameworks relevant to CI/CD include:

- **ISO/IEC 27001** – Information Security Management
- **SOC 2** – Service Organization Control Reports
- **PCI-DSS** – Payment Card Industry Data Security Standard
- **HIPAA** – Health Insurance Portability and Accountability Act
- **GDPR** – General Data Protection Regulation
- **FedRAMP** – Federal Risk and Authorization Management Program

Implementing Compliance in Azure DevOps Pipelines

Compliance must be embedded into every layer of the pipeline. Below are several strategies for achieving this using Azure DevOps.

1. Controlled Access and Role-Based Permissions

Restrict access to sensitive pipeline components, source code, and environments using **Role-Based Access Control (RBAC)**.

- Define roles like Reader, Contributor, Build Admin, and Project Admin.
- Assign least-privilege access per team or function.
- Use **Azure Active Directory** integration for SSO and MFA.

```
az devops security permission update \
  --subject user@company.com \
  --token repository \
  --permission-name "Edit build pipeline" \
  --allow false
```

Document access policies and enforce periodic reviews to align with compliance audits.

2. Code Change Traceability

CI/CD must ensure that every code change is traceable:

- Enforce **work** **item** **linking** in pull requests.

- Require **commit** **messages** to follow defined formats.

- Store metadata such as author, timestamp, branch, and reviewer.

Branch policy example:

- Enforce linking of work items

- Block PRs without associated tasks or bugs

- Require peer review for all changes

These traceability rules help demonstrate adherence to change management processes required by ISO and SOC 2.

3. Pipeline Templates for Standardization

Use reusable templates to enforce pipeline logic consistency across all teams:

```
# ci-template.yml

parameters:

  - name: runTests

    type: boolean

    default: true



steps:

  - task: InstallDependencies@1

  - task: BuildApp@1

  - ${{ if parameters.runTests }}:

      - task: RunTests@1

```

Teams extend this template and automatically inherit best practices. Templates should include logging, approval gates, artifact handling, and compliance controls.

Securing Artifacts and Releases

Build outputs and release packages must be treated as sensitive assets:

- Store artifacts in **Azure Artifacts** or a secure repository.

- Use **immutable build pipelines** to prevent tampering.

- Digitally sign artifacts where applicable.

- Define **retention policies** based on compliance rules (e.g., retain production builds for 7 years for financial audits).

```
- task: PublishBuildArtifacts@1

  inputs:

    artifactName: 'MyApp'

    publishLocation: 'Container'
```

Restrict download access and require authentication for consumption.

Managing Infrastructure as Code (IaC) Compliance

IaC ensures repeatable and auditable infrastructure provisioning. Azure DevOps supports Terraform, ARM, Bicep, and Ansible.

To ensure compliance:

- Validate IaC templates for security and cost

- Store templates in version-controlled repositories

- Automate scanning using tools like **Checkov, TFLint,** or **AzSK**

Example Checkov integration:

```
- script: |

    checkov -d ./infrastructure --quiet --framework terraform
```

```
displayName: 'Run Checkov Security Scan'
```

Any failed policy blocks the pipeline and sends alerts.

Enforcing Deployment Governance

Deployment pipelines must be tightly governed to meet compliance standards:

- **Use environment approvals** for regulated stages.
- Enforce **change request documentation** for production changes.
- Require sign-offs and implement **change windows**.

Azure DevOps supports:

- Manual approval gates
- Business hours restrictions
- Custom API checks

Example:

```
environments:

- name: 'Production'

  checks:

    - type: 'Approval'

      reviewers:

        - id: 'compliance@company.com'
```

This ensures that no deployment reaches production without explicit compliance review.

Audit and Monitoring for Compliance

Azure DevOps provides built-in auditing capabilities, but you should also integrate with central SIEM or compliance tools:

1. Azure DevOps Auditing

Track:

- Pipeline edits and executions
- Variable and secret changes
- Permission and role modifications
- User sign-ins and project activities

Export audit logs regularly and retain them for the duration mandated by compliance policies.

2. Log Aggregation

Forward logs to:

- **Azure** **Monitor**
- **Azure** **Sentinel**
- **Splunk**, **Elastic** **Stack**, or other SIEMs

This allows for centralized correlation, anomaly detection, and compliance reporting.

3. Compliance Dashboards

Build dashboards in Power BI or Azure Monitor to track:

- Failed policy checks
- Manual override usage
- Deployment volume per environment
- Audit events over time

Dashboards provide real-time visibility and help compliance officers identify gaps.

Data Protection and Privacy Compliance

CI/CD pipelines often handle sensitive user or customer data. You must protect this data during build, test, and deployment.

Key controls:

- **Mask** **PII** **or** **sensitive** **data** in logs
- Use **secure** **test** **data** in test pipelines
- Redact confidential fields from outputs
- Encrypt secrets in transit and at rest

Use Azure Key Vault for storing secrets, and avoid leaking data via logs or telemetry.

If data anonymization is required by law (e.g., GDPR), use synthetic or obfuscated test data in CI/CD environments.

Supporting Regulatory Compliance with Documentation

Documentation is essential for audit readiness. Maintain:

- Pipeline definitions and changes
- Access control policies
- Audit logs and incident responses
- Compliance approvals and artifacts
- Code promotion and rollback procedures

Use Azure DevOps Wiki or Confluence to maintain living documentation. Keep changelogs updated and store signed approvals for production changes.

Validating Compliance with Testing and Reporting

Compliance isn't a one-time activity—it must be validated regularly.

- Schedule automated **compliance** **tests** in your CI pipelines
- Perform **manual** **reviews** quarterly or before audits

- Use external tools like **Veracode**, **SonarQube**, or **Snyk** for vulnerability and license compliance scanning

Integrate these tools into your build jobs:

```
- task: SonarQubePrepare@4

- task: SonarQubeAnalyze@4

- task: SonarQubePublish@4
```

Generate reports and make them accessible to security and compliance teams.

Key Considerations for Global Enterprises

Global organizations must also consider:

- **Data residency laws** (e.g., host in EU for EU citizens)

- **Cross-border access controls**

- **Regional disaster recovery zones**

- **Localized compliance policies** for specific jurisdictions

Azure DevOps and Azure itself support multi-region deployments, geo-replication, and compliance certifications across regions.

Refer to the **Microsoft Trust Center** for region-specific compliance capabilities.

Summary

Compliance is no longer an afterthought—it's an essential part of modern DevOps workflows. With Azure DevOps, organizations can embed compliance controls directly into CI/CD pipelines without sacrificing agility.

Key takeaways:

- Enforce access controls and traceability

- Use templates and environment gates for governance
- Automate testing, scanning, and approvals
- Monitor everything and retain audit trails
- Document, report, and continuously improve compliance posture

By integrating compliance into the development lifecycle, teams can innovate securely, deploy confidently, and stay audit-ready at all times.

Best Practices for Secure Deployments

Secure deployments are not merely the result of writing secure code—they are the outcome of a pipeline and process designed with security in mind at every stage. From build to release, every aspect of your CI/CD lifecycle must adopt security best practices to safeguard applications, data, infrastructure, and end users.

In Azure DevOps, secure deployments involve the integration of access controls, secrets management, environment isolation, policy enforcement, compliance validation, and runtime protection into a unified deployment strategy. Let's explore the best practices that should be incorporated into every secure deployment pipeline.

Principle of Least Privilege

Start by ensuring that every user, service connection, and pipeline has only the access required—and nothing more.

- Restrict **write access** to production environments.
- Separate **build and deploy responsibilities** between teams.
- Use **scoped service connections** with minimal permissions.
- Enforce **role-based access controls (RBAC)** across projects, pipelines, variable groups, and libraries.

Use the Azure DevOps CLI to review and set permissions:

```
az devops security permission list \
  --subject user@company.com \
  --token project \
```

```
--output table
```

Regularly audit and revoke unused or excessive permissions.

Secure Service Connections

Service connections (for Azure, AWS, Docker, etc.) enable pipelines to deploy artifacts or infrastructure. These must be tightly controlled.

Best Practices:

- Use **managed identities** when possible (no secrets).

- Avoid personal access tokens (PATs) for production deployments.

- Set connections to be **approved for use by specific pipelines only**.

- Use **environment-scoped connections** and not organization-wide ones.

- Rotate credentials periodically and immediately after suspected compromise.

For example, to scope a service connection to a project:

```
az devops service-endpoint update \

  --id <serviceConnectionId> \

  --project MyProject \

  --enable-for-all false
```

Secure Build and Deployment Agents

Your build and deployment agents are critical security points—they interact directly with your code, credentials, and infrastructure.

For Microsoft-hosted agents:

- Benefit from Azure DevOps-managed isolation.

- Avoid caching sensitive data across jobs or builds.

For self-hosted agents:

- Run in **isolated, minimal-permission environments** (e.g., containers or locked-down VMs).

- Use ephemeral runners if possible to reduce persistence risk.

- Avoid storing secrets on disk.

- Regularly patch OS and tools used on the runner.

- Limit internet and network access as needed.

Secure the Deployment Pipeline

Design your pipeline to prevent injection, tampering, and privilege escalation.

Key practices:

- Avoid using `script: echo $(secret)` — secrets must never be logged.

- Use **pipeline templates** to centralize logic and restrict customization.

- Limit script execution permissions to trusted teams.

- Review pipeline definitions via pull requests and approval workflows.

- Validate pipeline definitions using tools like **YAML schema linters**.

Example:

```
variables:
  - group: SecureSecrets


jobs:
  - job: Deploy
    steps:
```

```
  - script: |

      echo "Deploying app version $(Build.BuildNumber)"

      ./deploy.sh --key $(mySecretKey)
```

In the above case, `mySecretKey` must be marked as a secret in Azure DevOps to avoid leaking it to logs.

Secrets Management

Secrets used in deployments—API keys, passwords, tokens—should never be hardcoded or passed insecurely.

Recommendations:

- Use **Azure Key Vault** to store and retrieve secrets securely.
- Mask secrets in logs automatically using Azure DevOps secret variables.
- Grant pipelines read-only access to the specific secrets they need.
- Regularly **rotate secrets** and expire unused ones.

Using Key Vault with variable groups:

1. Create a Key Vault and set access policies.
2. Link it to a variable group in Azure DevOps.
3. Use the secrets in YAML:

```
variables:

  - group: KeyVaultSecrets
```

Never expose secrets in inline scripts or configuration files.

Enforce Manual and Automated Approvals

Secure deployments often require **human oversight**. Azure DevOps allows manual and automated approvals for deployment stages.

Manual approvals:

- Use for critical stages (e.g., production).

- Define specific approvers (e.g., compliance team, SRE lead).

- Require justification and record approval comments.

Automated gates:

- Call an external API to validate compliance.

- Run security scanners.

- Perform health checks or vulnerability validation.

Example of a deployment environment with manual approval:

```
environments:

  - name: 'Production'

    checks:

      - approvals:

          reviewers:

            - id: 'leadengineer@company.com'
```

Environment Segregation

Separate environments to ensure that issues in one stage do not affect another.

Typical setup:

- Dev → QA → UAT → Staging → Production

Each environment should:

- Use different service connections or resource groups.

- Have separate access control policies.

- Be locked down progressively toward production.

- Use feature toggles or deployment rings to control exposure.

Avoid deploying the same artifacts to all environments unless tested in preceding stages.

Immutable Infrastructure and Configuration as Code

Immutable infrastructure means that infrastructure and environments are **not modified in-place**, but rather replaced when changes occur.

Use tools like:

- Terraform

- ARM/Bicep templates

- Pulumi

- Ansible

Benefits:

- Easy rollback

- Better auditability

- Consistent, repeatable deployments

CI/CD integration example:

```
- task: TerraformCLI@0
  inputs:
    provider: 'azurerm'
    command: 'apply'
    environmentServiceName: 'AzureConnection'
```

Also apply **configuration as code** for app settings, feature flags, and environment variables.

Deploy with Verification

Always validate the success and integrity of a deployment before considering it complete.

Techniques:

- Health probes or synthetic tests after deployment
- Smoke tests and endpoint validation
- Real-time alert monitoring (e.g., Azure Monitor, App Insights)
- Use of release gates that block progression until tests pass

In Azure DevOps, post-deployment scripts and probes can be used to run these checks automatically.

Example:

```
- script: |
    curl -f https://myapp.azurewebsites.net/health || exit 1
```

Failing the step will prevent the next stage from executing.

Rollback Strategies

Not all deployments go as planned—secure deployments must include a **well-defined rollback plan**.

Options include:

- **Canary deployments**: release to a small subset of users first.
- **Blue/Green deployments**: deploy to an idle environment, then switch traffic.
- **Feature flags**: disable faulty features without code changes.

- **Versioned releases**: deploy new versions alongside existing ones.

Azure DevOps does not manage rollbacks automatically—you must script this logic into your pipeline.

Logging and Auditing

Enable detailed logging and retain it for an appropriate duration to support forensics, compliance, and debugging.

Ensure that:

- All deployment actions are logged.
- Secrets are never printed.
- Logs are sent to centralized storage.
- Access to logs is controlled and auditable.

You can send logs to:

- Azure Monitor
- Log Analytics
- Microsoft Sentinel
- External SIEM solutions (e.g., Splunk, ELK)

Maintain audit trails for:

- Pipeline changes
- Environment access
- Deployment approvals
- Service connection use

Secure Your Dependencies

Many attacks exploit third-party libraries. Secure deployment pipelines should:

- **Scan** **dependencies** for vulnerabilities.

- Maintain **allowlists** of approved libraries.

- Block builds if critical issues are found.

Integrate tools like:

- Snyk

- WhiteSource

- SonarQube

- OWASP Dependency-Check

Azure DevOps Marketplace also has extensions for automatic scanning.

Zero Trust Deployment Model

Adopt a **zero trust** model for your CI/CD environment:

- Assume breach—validate everything.

- Require identity verification for each action.

- Encrypt communication between systems.

- Validate pipeline artifacts with signatures or checksums.

- Avoid shared or persistent secrets.

This mindset enhances the security of your overall deployment process.

Summary

Secure deployments in Azure DevOps are achieved by building a pipeline that is transparent, auditable, isolated, and policy-driven. Following best practices reduces the risk of deployment-time vulnerabilities and ensures the integrity of your applications in production.

Key takeaways:

- Enforce RBAC and least privilege everywhere.
- Store secrets securely and avoid leaks in logs.
- Require manual and automated approvals for critical stages.
- Segment and lock down environments based on stage.
- Use immutable infrastructure and configuration as code.
- Verify deployments post-release and implement robust rollback plans.
- Integrate security testing and dependency scanning into your CI/CD pipeline.
- Adopt a zero trust mindset in every layer of deployment.

By incorporating these best practices, you can create a secure, scalable, and compliant deployment process that supports rapid innovation without compromising safety.

Chapter 8: Monitoring and Troubleshooting CI/CD Pipelines

Logging and Telemetry in Pipelines

Effective monitoring and troubleshooting of CI/CD pipelines is essential for maintaining healthy DevOps workflows. Azure DevOps offers a robust suite of logging, telemetry, and diagnostic tools that allow developers and operations teams to track every aspect of their pipelines. This section explores in-depth techniques for utilizing these tools to identify, prevent, and resolve issues in CI/CD pipelines.

Understanding the Importance of Logging and Telemetry

Logging and telemetry are critical components of a modern CI/CD strategy. Logging refers to the recording of discrete events during the execution of a process, such as build steps, test results, deployment events, and errors. Telemetry, on the other hand, involves the collection of real-time metrics and insights about system behavior, usage patterns, and performance.

When implemented effectively, these tools provide visibility into the pipeline's performance, helping teams:

- Identify root causes of failures quickly.

- Improve the reliability and resilience of deployment processes.

- Make data-driven decisions for continuous improvement.

- Ensure compliance and auditability.

Types of Logs in Azure DevOps

Azure DevOps provides several types of logs across various stages of the CI/CD pipeline:

- **Build Logs**: Generated during the execution of a CI pipeline. These logs include task execution details, success/failure states, and output from scripts or tools.

- **Release Logs**: Captured during CD pipeline execution, showing deployment progress, agent logs, and error messages.

- **Agent Diagnostic Logs**: Useful for debugging issues related to the Azure Pipelines agents themselves.

- **Audit Logs**: Maintain a historical record of changes to projects, pipelines, permissions, and other configurations for compliance and tracking.

Enabling Detailed Logging

By default, Azure DevOps provides comprehensive logs for all pipelines. However, in complex environments, you may need to enable enhanced logging for deeper insights.

To enable verbose logging in a pipeline, you can use the `System.Debug` variable:

```
variables:

  System.Debug: true
```

Setting `System.Debug` to `true` increases the verbosity of logs, displaying internal operations of tasks and service connections, which is especially useful for debugging authentication or connection issues.

Integrating Telemetry with Azure Monitor

Azure Monitor is a powerful observability tool that allows you to collect, analyze, and act on telemetry data from Azure DevOps, apps, and infrastructure. You can configure Azure DevOps to send logs and metrics to Azure Monitor using diagnostic settings and the REST API.

Steps to integrate Azure DevOps with Azure Monitor:

1. **Enable Diagnostic Settings:**

   - Navigate to Project Settings → Diagnostic Settings.

   - Choose the Azure Monitor destination (Log Analytics, Event Hub, or Storage Account).

   - Select the log types to export (Audit logs, Pipelines, etc.).

2. **Configure Azure Monitor Alerts:**

   - Use Log Analytics queries to define metrics thresholds.

   - Set up alert rules based on these queries.

   - Configure action groups to notify stakeholders or trigger automated responses.

Sample Log Analytics query:

```
AzureDevOpsAuditing

| where OperationName == "RunPipeline"

| where ResultDescription != "Succeeded"

| project TimeGenerated, OperationName, ResultDescription, ActorUPN,
ProjectName
```

This query shows all failed pipeline executions across projects.

Custom Logging with Scripts

Custom scripts (PowerShell, Bash, etc.) are commonly used in pipelines. It's crucial to ensure these scripts generate logs in a format that can be parsed and understood easily.

Azure Pipelines supports specific logging commands that enable developers to control how messages appear in the logs:

- `##vso[task.logissue]` – Log warnings and errors.

- `##vso[task.debug]` – Log debug messages when `System.Debug` is enabled.

- `##vso[task.setvariable]` – Log and set variables dynamically.

Example: PowerShell custom log message

```
Write-Output "##vso[task.logissue type=error]Deployment failed due to
missing configuration."
```

Example: Bash script with logging

```
echo "##vso[task.logissue type=warning]This step may impact future
builds."
```

These commands help surface important messages in the pipeline logs and make it easier to find relevant information during troubleshooting.

Using Pipeline Analytics

Azure DevOps includes a built-in analytics extension that allows users to create custom dashboards and reports about pipeline performance, failure trends, build durations, and more.

Key capabilities:

- **Success Rate Analysis**: Monitor pass/fail rates across branches or stages.

- **Build Duration Analysis**: Identify steps that consume the most time.

- **Failure Hotspots**: Highlight recurring failure points.

You can access analytics under "Project Settings → Analytics views" and connect to tools like Power BI to build comprehensive visual reports.

Sample Power BI report ideas:

- Deployment frequency by environment.

- Mean time to recovery (MTTR) after failures.

- Lead time for changes from commit to production.

Troubleshooting Build Failures with Logs

When a build fails, it's important to follow a structured troubleshooting process:

1. **Start with the Error Message:**
   - Identify the exact step or task that failed.
   - Review any error codes or stack traces.

2. **Enable Debug Logging:**
   - If not already active, enable `System.Debug: true`.

3. **Check Dependencies:**
   - Ensure external dependencies (e.g., NuGet, NPM) are available.
   - Verify that environment variables or secrets are correctly configured.

4. **Agent Logs:**
   - Look at the pipeline agent logs if the issue appears to be infrastructure-related.

- o Use self-hosted agents' logs if hosted in custom environments.

5. **Compare** **with** **Working** **Builds**:

- o Use the "Compare" feature in the pipeline UI to check differences between successful and failed runs.

6. **Use** **Test** **and** **Coverage** **Reports**:

- o Analyze failed test logs and code coverage to understand issues in unit or integration tests.

Implementing Centralized Logging Strategies

In complex environments with multiple pipelines, services, and teams, centralized logging becomes essential.

Best practices:

- **Log aggregation**: Send logs from all pipelines to a central repository (e.g., Azure Log Analytics, Elastic Stack).

- **Standardized formats**: Use structured logging (e.g., JSON) for better parsing and indexing.

- **Retention policies**: Define log retention based on compliance and performance needs.

- **Tagging and metadata**: Use consistent tags (e.g., pipeline name, stage, environment) to categorize logs effectively.

Logging for Compliance and Auditability

For regulated industries (e.g., healthcare, finance), logging is not just about debugging—it's a compliance requirement. Azure DevOps supports audit logging and traceability for all pipeline activities.

- **Audit Trails**: Capture who triggered which pipeline, when, and with what changes.

- **Change Logs**: Record configuration changes to YAML files and release definitions.

- **Role-Based Access Control (RBAC)**: Restrict who can view or edit logs based on roles.

Ensure that logs are retained according to organizational and legal policies. Integrate with security information and event management (SIEM) tools for real-time monitoring and incident response.

Summary

Logging and telemetry form the backbone of effective CI/CD monitoring. Azure DevOps provides a mature logging framework, enriched by integrations with Azure Monitor and external systems. By understanding how to configure and utilize logs, create custom telemetry, and integrate analytics, teams can build a resilient, transparent, and traceable DevOps process.

In the next section, we'll dive into diagnosing build failures and deployment issues—transforming the data from logging and telemetry into actionable insights.

Diagnosing Build Failures and Deployment Issues

Diagnosing issues in CI/CD pipelines is one of the most vital skills for any DevOps engineer or software team. Failures can arise from a variety of sources—code defects, infrastructure problems, configuration mismatches, or external service disruptions. This section will provide a comprehensive strategy for identifying, investigating, and resolving failures in both build and deployment stages of your pipelines in Azure DevOps.

Common Causes of Pipeline Failures

Understanding the most frequent causes of pipeline failures is the first step toward effective diagnosis. These can be broadly categorized as:

- **Code-related issues**: Syntax errors, test failures, compilation errors, or logic bugs.

- **Dependency problems**: Missing or outdated packages, API schema mismatches, broken external services.

- **Infrastructure issues**: Insufficient resources, agent timeouts, file system permissions, or environment configuration problems.

- **Misconfiguration**: Incorrect YAML syntax, misused variables, or invalid task parameters.

- **Authentication and security**: Invalid service connections, expired tokens, or missing secrets.

Each of these causes presents different symptoms, and diagnosing them effectively requires both contextual knowledge and a systematic approach.

Building a Diagnosis Workflow

When a pipeline fails, a structured workflow helps minimize time spent troubleshooting:

1. **Identify** the **Stage** and **Step** of **Failure**

2. **Read** the **Logs** in **Detail**

3. **Analyze** **Inputs** and **Outputs**

4. **Check** **Pipeline** **History**

5. **Test** in **Isolation**

6. **Validate** **External** **Dependencies**

7. **Check** **Agent** **Health** and **Configuration**

8. **Collaborate** and **Share** **Context**

Let's explore each of these steps with practical tips and examples.

Step 1: Identify the Stage and Step of Failure

Azure DevOps provides a clear visual breakdown of each stage and job in your pipeline. Use this to locate the exact job and task that failed.

- Navigate to the failed pipeline run.

- Expand the failed stage and drill down into the task logs.

- Note the exact task name and error message.

This initial pinpointing helps rule out unrelated pipeline components.

Step 2: Read the Logs in Detail

Logs are your primary tool for understanding what went wrong. Look for:

- **Red-colored lines** indicating task failure.

- **Stack traces** or error codes.

- **Environment variables** and secrets (watch for redacted fields).

- **Exit codes** from scripts or build tools.

Example Log Output:

```
##[error]The nuget command failed with exit code(1) and error(MSBUILD
: error MSB1009: Project file does not exist.

Switch: MyApp.csproj)
```

In this case, the cause is a missing or misnamed project file. The resolution might involve fixing the path or updating the YAML task definition.

Step 3: Analyze Inputs and Outputs

Many tasks depend on variables, outputs from previous steps, or conditions.

For instance, if a build task fails due to a missing artifact, check whether:

- The artifact was created in an earlier stage.

- The output path is correct.

- Conditional execution logic is preventing prior tasks from running.

YAML snippet with conditional logic:

```
- task: PublishBuildArtifacts@1

  condition: succeeded()

  inputs:

    PathtoPublish: '$(Build.ArtifactStagingDirectory)'

    ArtifactName: 'drop'
```

Ensure that the condition matches the desired logic. If a prior task is skipped, dependent steps may also be skipped or fail.

Step 4: Check Pipeline History

Compare the failed run to previous successful runs.

- Use the **"Compare"** tab in the pipeline run summary.

- Look for changes in commit SHA, YAML definition, or parameters.

- Pay attention to tool version updates or configuration changes.

Sometimes, the error originates from a seemingly minor change—like a library version bump—that has unintended side effects.

Step 5: Test in Isolation

If a task or script is failing, test it locally or in a sandbox environment.

Example: Failing Bash script

Pipeline log:

```
##[error]./deploy.sh: line 45: kubectl: command not found
```

Testing locally may reveal that the task requires a self-hosted agent with `kubectl` installed. Either update the agent or use a container-based task that includes the necessary tools.

YAML fix:

```
- task: Bash@3
  inputs:
    targetType: 'inline'
    script: |
      echo "Running deployment"
      sudo apt-get install -y kubectl
      ./deploy.sh
```

Step 6: Validate External Dependencies

Pipelines often rely on:

- Package registries (NuGet, NPM)
- REST APIs or third-party services
- Secrets stored in Azure Key Vault

Issues may include:

- Rate   limits

- DNS   resolution   problems

- Expired   secrets

Use retries, fallbacks, or mocks where feasible.

YAML with retry:

```
- task: Bash@3
  inputs:
    script: |
      for i in {1..3}; do
        curl https://external-api.com/deploy && break || sleep 10
      done
```

Secrets stored in Key Vault should be monitored and rotated regularly:

```
- task: AzureKeyVault@2
  inputs:
    azureSubscription: 'MyServiceConnection'
    KeyVaultName: 'my-keyvault'
    SecretsFilter: '*'
```

Step 7: Check Agent Health and Configuration

Problems sometimes arise from the build agent itself:

- Disk   space   full

- Missing   tools

- Network   issues

- Permissions   errors

Azure DevOps provides hosted agents with standard toolchains, but self-hosted agents require maintenance. Run diagnostic commands at the start of the job to confirm environment state:

```
- script: |

    echo "Checking disk space..."

    df -h

    echo "Checking installed tools..."

    node -v

    dotnet --info

  displayName: 'Environment Diagnostics'
```

If the environment appears incorrect, ensure the correct agent pool is being used:

```
pool:

  name: 'MyCustomAgentPool'
```

Step 8: Collaborate and Share Context

When facing persistent or unfamiliar issues, share logs and context with team members. Use:

- Azure   DevOps   comments   on   failed   runs.

- Markdown   annotations   in   work   items.

- Integration   with   Teams   or   Slack   to   alert   about   failed   builds.

Use tags or metadata to group pipeline runs by feature, team, or release. This makes it easier to spot recurring issues or regressions.

```
- task: Bash@3
```

```
name: 'TagRun'

inputs:

  targetType: 'inline'

  script: |

    echo "##vso[build.addbuildtag]FeatureX"
```

Advanced Diagnostic Techniques

Dependency Caching Analysis

Builds that fail intermittently may be affected by caching mechanisms. Caches should be scoped correctly:

```
- task: Cache@2

  inputs:

    key: 'npm | "$(Agent.OS)" | package-lock.json'

    path: $(Pipeline.Workspace)/.npm
```

Ensure keys are accurate and not overbroad, which could result in using outdated dependencies.

Debugging Multi-Stage Pipelines

Failures in one stage might cascade. Use `dependsOn` and `condition` attributes wisely:

```
stages:

  - stage: Build

    jobs:

      - job: BuildJob

        ...

  - stage: Test

    dependsOn: Build
```

```
condition: succeeded('Build')

jobs:

  - job: TestJob

    ...
```

Missing dependencies or incorrect conditional logic can cause stages to skip or run erroneously.

Using Diagnostic Mode

When builds fail with unclear reasons, diagnostic mode can help.

- Enable debug logging (System.Debug: true).

- Add additional logging to scripts.

- Output environment variables:

```
- script: printenv

  displayName: 'Print Environment Variables'
```

Be cautious not to expose secrets in logs.

Conclusion

Diagnosing build and deployment issues is a multifaceted task that requires a disciplined approach. Azure DevOps provides rich tooling to aid in this process—from detailed logs to diagnostic tasks and external integrations. By following a structured process, testing in isolation, leveraging logs effectively, and validating assumptions at each stage, teams can significantly reduce downtime, improve developer confidence, and ship changes faster.

In the next section, we'll explore how to proactively alert and respond to pipeline issues to ensure rapid recovery and business continuity.

Alerting and Incident Response

An effective CI/CD strategy goes beyond just building and deploying code—it must also include robust mechanisms for alerting and incident response. When something goes wrong in a pipeline, a rapid response can mean the difference between a minor hiccup and a prolonged outage. This section delves into building resilient alerting systems, setting up proactive monitoring, and forming a mature incident response workflow within Azure DevOps and integrated tools.

The Role of Alerting in CI/CD

Alerting is the first step in incident response. The goal is to notify the right people as quickly and clearly as possible when something breaks. In a CI/CD pipeline, alerts can be triggered by:

- Failed   builds   or   deployments
- Missed   schedules   (for   timed   pipelines)
- Performance   degradation   (e.g.,   slow   builds)
- Flaky   or   failed   tests
- Security   or   compliance   violations
- Infrastructure   errors   (e.g.,   low   disk   space   on   agents)

Proper alerting enables:

- **Immediate   awareness   of   issues**
- **Faster   MTTR   (Mean   Time   to   Recovery)**
- **Better   accountability   and   post-mortems**
- **Improved   team   coordination   during   incidents**

Alerting Tools and Channels

Azure DevOps integrates with multiple tools and services to send alerts. Key options include:

- **Azure   Monitor**: Centralized   monitoring   and   alerting   platform
- **Service Hooks**: Custom outbound notifications to tools like Slack, Microsoft Teams, or   custom   webhooks
- **Email   Notifications**: Built-in   notification   system   for   pipeline   events
- **REST   APIs**: Trigger   alerts   programmatically   using   scripts   or   custom   tools

- **Work Item Rules**: Automatically create bugs or tasks when conditions are met

Example: Email Notification on Pipeline Failure

1. Navigate to **Project Settings** → **Notifications**

2. Select **New Subscription**

3. Choose **Build completed** as the event

4. Filter to **Failed builds**

5. Add users or groups to notify

You can fine-tune subscriptions by project, branch, result status, and more.

Using Azure Monitor for CI/CD Alerts

Azure Monitor can be integrated directly with Azure DevOps to create detailed alerts. It supports metric and log-based alerting, which allows for complex conditions and thresholds.

Steps to Set Up Alerting:

1. **Send Logs to Azure Monitor**

   - Enable diagnostic settings in Azure DevOps.

   - Export logs to a Log Analytics workspace.

2. **Create Log Analytics Queries**

   - Use Kusto Query Language (KQL) to define failure conditions.

3. **Define Alert Rules**

   - Attach queries to alert rules.

   - Set thresholds, time aggregation, and frequency.

4. **Add Action Groups**

   - Configure emails, SMS, webhooks, or automation runbooks to execute when alerts trigger.

Sample KQL for Failed Pipelines:

```
AzureDevOpsAuditing

| where OperationName == "RunPipeline"

| where ResultDescription != "Succeeded"

| summarize count() by bin(TimeGenerated, 5m), ProjectName
```

This query triggers an alert if there are repeated pipeline failures in a 5-minute window.

Creating Custom Webhooks for Real-Time Alerts

Webhooks can be used to push real-time notifications to any HTTP endpoint when a pipeline event occurs.

Example: Notify a Slack Channel

1. Create a Slack Webhook URL.

2. Go to **Project Settings** → **Service Hooks**

3. Create a new hook for **Build completed**

4. Set filters for **Result** = **Failed**

5. Paste the webhook URL and configure the payload

Slack will receive formatted messages every time a pipeline fails.

Example Payload:

```
{

  "text": "🖥 Build failed for project *MyApp* on branch *main*. Check the logs here: https://dev.azure.com/org/project/_build/results?buildId=1234"

}
```

This method is especially useful in DevOps war rooms and real-time debugging sessions.

Implementing Incident Response Workflow

Once an alert is received, it triggers the incident response process. A well-structured workflow helps teams address the issue effectively and consistently.

Core Phases of Incident Response:

1. **Detection** – Triggered by alerts

2. **Triage** – Assess severity and impact

3. **Assignment** – Notify on-call engineer or response team

4. **Resolution** – Fix the issue or roll back changes

5. **Post-Mortem** – Analyze root cause and document lessons learned

Triage Process:

- Is this a known issue?

- Is it isolated or systemic?

- Is there a recent code/config change?

- Can the pipeline be manually rerun?

Use automation where possible to assist in triage:

```
- script: |

  echo "##[group]Auto-diagnosis"

  printenv

  df -h

  cat logs/errors.log || true

  echo "##[endgroup]"
```

Automating Incident Response

Advanced teams automate parts of the response process using tools like:

- **Azure Logic Apps**: Trigger actions like rollback, scaling, or notifications

- **Power Automate**: Integrate pipeline events with Microsoft 365 tools

- **GitHub Actions**: Run scripts across repos when alerts occur

Example: Automatic Work Item Creation on Failure

```
- task: AzureCLI@2

  inputs:

    azureSubscription: 'MyServiceConnection'

    scriptType: bash

    scriptLocation: inlineScript

    inlineScript: |

      az boards work-item create \

        --title "CI Pipeline Failed - $(Build.DefinitionName)" \

        --type "Bug" \

        --project "MyProject" \

        --description "Pipeline ID: $(Build.BuildId)"
```

This ensures every failure is tracked for accountability and follow-up.

Setting On-Call Rotations

During off-hours, alerts need to reach someone available to respond. Azure DevOps doesn't have built-in on-call management, but it integrates well with tools like:

- **PagerDuty**

- **Opsgenie**

- **VictorOps**

These platforms provide:

- Dynamic   scheduling

- Escalation policies
- Acknowledgment tracking
- Integrations with Azure Monitor and webhooks

Building a Response Culture

Technology alone isn't enough—organizations must foster a culture where:

- Incidents are viewed as learning opportunities, not blame events
- Post-mortems are standard practice
- Knowledge sharing is encouraged
- Alerts are fine-tuned to reduce noise

A high volume of unactionable alerts can desensitize teams, leading to alert fatigue. Use the following principles:

- **Only alert on actionable conditions**
- **Set severity levels** (e.g., info, warning, critical)
- **Throttle alerts** to avoid flooding inboxes
- **Suppress alerts during known outages or maintenance**

Alert Testing and Simulation

Regularly test your alerting system:

- Trigger test failures in a pipeline
- Ensure alerts are received by the correct team
- Simulate escalation paths and recovery plans
- Document all steps taken and verify accuracy

Use Azure DevOps pipeline stages for testing:

```
stages:
```

```
- stage: SimulateFailure

  jobs:

    - job: FailJob

      steps:

        - script: exit 1
          displayName: 'Simulate failure for alert test'
```

Make sure that alerting systems pick up this failure and that response documentation is followed.

Summary

Robust alerting and incident response are foundational to a mature DevOps culture. Azure DevOps, combined with tools like Azure Monitor, Slack, and PagerDuty, provides the framework to detect issues early, notify the right stakeholders, and resolve problems efficiently. By automating incident workflows, managing alert noise, and building a proactive team culture, organizations can reduce downtime, improve resilience, and continuously improve their CI/CD processes.

In the next section, we will look at continuous improvement strategies that help refine your CI/CD workflows and prevent future incidents before they occur.

Continuous Improvement Strategies

Continuous improvement is at the heart of modern DevOps practices. In the context of CI/CD pipelines, it means constantly analyzing performance, identifying bottlenecks, resolving recurring issues, enhancing security, and refining processes to reduce waste and increase software delivery speed and quality. A well-oiled pipeline is not a static construct—it evolves. This section focuses on actionable strategies, practical metrics, and cultural shifts required to sustain and evolve CI/CD pipelines through continuous improvement.

The Philosophy of Continuous Improvement

Continuous improvement is inspired by principles from Lean, Agile, and DevOps cultures. It promotes:

- **Small, incremental changes over time**
- **Early and frequent feedback**

- Embracing failure as a learning opportunity

- Team collaboration across silos

- Data-driven decision making

In a CI/CD context, continuous improvement applies to both the *product* and the *pipeline* that delivers it.

Establishing Baseline Metrics

Before improving anything, you must measure it. Establishing baseline performance metrics allows teams to identify trends and assess the impact of improvements.

Some critical CI/CD metrics include:

- **Deployment Frequency**: How often code is deployed to production

- **Lead Time for Changes**: Time from code commit to deployment

- **Change Failure Rate**: Percentage of deployments that result in failure

- **Mean Time to Recovery (MTTR)**: Time taken to restore service after failure

- **Pipeline Duration**: How long the full pipeline takes to execute

- **Test Coverage and Flakiness**: Stability and reliability of the test suite

Using Azure DevOps Analytics for Metrics

Azure DevOps provides built-in analytics views. You can export this data to Power BI for visualization or use the REST API to retrieve it programmatically.

Sample REST API call to get build metrics:

```
GET
https://dev.azure.com/{organization}/{project}/_apis/build/builds?api-version=6.0
```

Filter and analyze this data to establish averages, identify outliers, and monitor trends.

Feedback Loops and Retrospectives

CI/CD pipelines generate immense feedback: logs, alerts, test results, code quality scans, and deployment success/failure rates. However, feedback is only valuable when acted upon.

Implement Regular Retrospectives

Hold retrospectives after:

- Major incidents
- Significant releases
- Regular time intervals (e.g., biweekly)

Ask key questions:

- What went well?
- What didn't go as expected?
- What did we learn?
- What will we change moving forward?

Track and follow up on action items in your backlog or Kanban board.

Improving Pipeline Speed and Efficiency

A sluggish pipeline delays feedback, frustrates developers, and encourages risky workarounds. Common causes of slow pipelines:

- Redundant tasks
- Poorly scoped caches
- Sequential jobs that could run in parallel
- Heavy or unnecessary tests

Strategies to Optimize Pipeline Performance

1. **Parallelization**

Split jobs into parallel units where possible:

```
jobs:

  - job: BuildFrontend
```

```
  ...

- job: BuildBackend

  ...
```

2. Selective   Builds

Only build what's changed. Use path filters:

```
trigger:

  paths:

    include:

      - 'src/frontend/*'
```

3. Use   Pipeline   Caching

Cache dependencies like NPM or NuGet packages:

```
- task: Cache@2

  inputs:

    key: 'npm | "$(Agent.OS)" | package-lock.json'

    path: $(Pipeline.Workspace)/.npm
```

4. Pre-built   Images   or   Containers

Use pre-baked build agents or containers with required tools already installed, reducing setup time.

5. Fail   Fast

Run quick validation tasks first (e.g., linting), and halt early if they fail. This prevents wasting time on later stages.

Test Quality and Coverage

Automated testing is the backbone of CI/CD. However, not all tests are equal in value. Over time, test suites can become brittle, slow, and unreliable.

Improve Test Signal-to-Noise Ratio

- **Eliminate flaky tests**: Track failed tests and prioritize stabilization.

- **Tag and categorize**: Separate unit, integration, and end-to-end tests.

- **Run by impact**: Use test impact analysis to only run tests affected by recent changes.

- **Parallelize test execution**: Distribute across agents or containers.

Example: Running tagged tests only

```
- script: |

    pytest -m "smoke"

  displayName: 'Run Smoke Tests'
```

Track Code Coverage

Use tools like Coverlet (for .NET), Jest (JavaScript), or JaCoCo (Java). Publish coverage reports and establish a minimum threshold.

```
- task: PublishCodeCoverageResults@1

  inputs:

    codeCoverageTool: 'Cobertura'

    summaryFileLocation: '$(Build.SourcesDirectory)/coverage.xml'
```

Security as a Continuous Concern

Security must be baked into CI/CD, not bolted on at the end.

Secure Development Lifecycle (SDL) Integration

- Run **static analysis (SAST)** as part of the build.

- Run **dependency checks** using tools like `OWASP Dependency-Check`, `npm audit`, or `dotnet list package --vulnerable`.

- Use **secret scanning tools** to detect API keys and credentials in code.

Example: Secret detection

```
- task: Bash@3
  inputs:
    script: |
      trufflehog filesystem --directory ./src --json
```

Enforce Policies with Azure DevOps

Use branch policies to require:

- PR reviews

- Successful build validation

- Linting or formatting checks

- Status checks from security tools

Shifting Left with Observability

Observability traditionally focused on production systems. However, incorporating observability in CI/CD leads to earlier detection of problems.

Metrics to Monitor During CI/CD

- Number of builds per day

- Build queue times

- Agent usage and concurrency

- Test flakiness rate

- Deployment frequency

Use dashboards to visualize these and drive conversations in standups and retrospectives.

Integrate Monitoring Tools

Connect Azure Pipelines with tools like:

- Azure   Monitor

- Application   Insights

- Grafana   or   Kibana   (via   Log   Analytics)

- Custom   dashboards   in   Power   BI

Automating Improvements and Remediation

Where feasible, automate improvements:

- **Auto-format code** using Prettier, Black, or dotnet format

- **Auto-create bugs** for failing pipelines

- **Auto-retry transient failures**

Retry example using bash loop:

```
for i in {1..3}; do
  npm install && break || sleep 10
done
```

This helps stabilize pipelines impacted by flaky networks or external services.

Encouraging a Culture of Experimentation

To continuously improve, teams need psychological safety and autonomy to experiment.

- **A/B test pipeline configurations**

- **Try canary deployments or feature flags**

- **Run pilot projects with new tools**

Share learnings in internal tech talks or documentation portals.

Make pipeline YAML files part of code review processes, so everyone is empowered to improve CI/CD processes.

Documenting and Versioning Pipelines

Track changes to pipeline configurations just like application code. Use:

- Separate folders for CI/CD YAMLs
- Naming conventions for clarity
- Semantic versioning if pipelines are used across projects
- README files that explain each step

Pipeline repository layout example:

```
/ci
  build.yaml
  deploy.yaml
  README.md
  /templates
    node-build.yml
    dotnet-build.yml
```

Store templates for reusability and maintainability.

Post-Incident Reviews and RCA

Every pipeline incident is a chance to learn.

- Conduct **blameless** **postmortems**
- Perform **root** **cause** **analysis** **(RCA)**
- Document **timeline** **and** **response**

- Assign   follow-up   tasks

Track these in a shared knowledge base to reduce repeat occurrences.

Summary

Continuous improvement in CI/CD pipelines is a journey, not a destination. By measuring performance, soliciting feedback, optimizing bottlenecks, integrating security, and fostering a learning culture, teams can deliver software faster, safer, and more efficiently. Azure DevOps, with its extensibility and ecosystem, offers powerful tools to support this evolution.

In the next chapter, we'll examine real-world use cases and case studies that bring together all the practices discussed so far—illustrating how top-performing teams build, run, and scale DevOps pipelines in production environments.

Chapter 9: Real-World Use Cases and Case Studies

CI/CD for Microservices

The rise of microservices architecture has transformed how software systems are designed, built, and deployed. CI/CD plays a critical role in enabling scalable, independent, and rapid deployment of microservices. In this section, we explore how Azure DevOps supports CI/CD workflows tailored for microservices, addressing common challenges and providing practical strategies for success.

Microservices Overview and Deployment Challenges

Microservices break down monolithic applications into smaller, self-contained services that communicate over standard protocols like HTTP or messaging queues. Each service is independently deployable, often managed by a dedicated team, and typically has its own database or persistent store.

However, the independence of microservices introduces complexity in deployment:

- **Service Coordination**: Services may depend on one another, requiring careful orchestration.

- **Version Management**: Backward compatibility and versioning must be maintained.

- **Environment Configuration**: Each service may have unique deployment environments and variables.

- **Monitoring and Debugging**: Distributed logs and telemetry data need centralized visibility.

CI/CD addresses these challenges by automating build, test, and deployment processes, and Azure DevOps offers powerful tools to achieve this at scale.

Structuring a Repository for Microservices

Azure DevOps supports both **monorepo** and **polyrepo** strategies for managing microservices:

- **Monorepo**: All microservices reside in a single repository. This allows easy cross-service refactoring but may result in long build times.

- **Polyrepo**: Each service has its own repository. This enforces team autonomy and reduces build scope.

In practice, a hybrid approach is often used—services are grouped logically (e.g., by domain) within larger repositories.

Here's an example structure for a polyrepo setup:

```
/orders-service

  /src

  azure-pipelines.yml

/payments-service

  /src

  azure-pipelines.yml

/inventory-service

  /src

  azure-pipelines.yml
```

Each service has its own pipeline configuration, making them independently buildable and deployable.

CI Pipeline for a Microservice

Let's define a sample Azure DevOps pipeline for the `orders-service`. This pipeline includes source checkout, dependency restoration, build, test, and artifact publishing.

```
trigger:

  branches:

    include:

      - main


pool:

  vmImage: 'ubuntu-latest'
```

```yaml
variables:

  buildConfiguration: 'Release'


steps:

- task: UseDotNet@2

  inputs:

    packageType: 'sdk'

    version: '7.x'

    installationPath: $(Agent.ToolsDirectory)/dotnet


- task: DotNetCoreCLI@2

  inputs:

    command: 'restore'

    projects: '**/*.csproj'


- task: DotNetCoreCLI@2

  inputs:

    command: 'build'

    projects: '**/*.csproj'

    arguments: '--configuration $(buildConfiguration)'


- task: DotNetCoreCLI@2

  inputs:

    command: 'test'
```

```
  projects: '**/*Tests.csproj'

  arguments: '--configuration $(buildConfiguration) --logger trx'


- task: PublishBuildArtifacts@1

  inputs:

    PathtoPublish: '$(Build.ArtifactStagingDirectory)'

    ArtifactName: 'orders-service'
```

This pipeline can be adapted per service with minimal changes.

Multi-Service Deployment Strategies

Deployment strategies for microservices must account for their loosely coupled nature. Azure DevOps supports several strategies:

- **Independent Deployments**: Each service has its own release pipeline triggered by changes to its codebase.

- **Coordinated Deployments**: A parent pipeline coordinates deployment across multiple services, often via stages.

An example of a multi-service release pipeline:

```
stages:

- stage: BuildOrders

  jobs:

  - job: BuildOrdersJob

    steps:

    - template: pipelines/orders-build.yml


- stage: BuildPayments

  jobs:
```

```
  - job: BuildPaymentsJob

    steps:

      - template: pipelines/payments-build.yml


- stage: Deploy

  dependsOn: [BuildOrders, BuildPayments]

  jobs:

  - deployment: DeployToStaging

    environment: 'staging'

    strategy:

      runOnce:

        deploy:

          steps:

            - task: AzureWebApp@1

              inputs:

                appName: 'orders-api-staging'

                package: '$(Pipeline.Workspace)/orders-service/*.zip'
```

Containerization and Kubernetes

Containerization is commonly used with microservices to ensure environment parity. Azure DevOps integrates with Docker and Kubernetes to build and deploy containerized services.

A simplified example of a Docker build task in an Azure pipeline:

```
- task: Docker@2

  inputs:

    containerRegistry: 'MyACR'
```

```
    repository: 'orders-service'

    command: 'buildAndPush'

    Dockerfile: '**/Dockerfile'

    tags: |

      $(Build.BuildId)
```

Kubernetes deployments can be managed using `kubectl` tasks or Helm charts:

```
- task: Kubernetes@1

  inputs:

    connectionType: 'Azure Resource Manager'

    azureSubscription: 'MyAzureSub'

    azureResourceGroup: 'microservices-rg'

    kubernetesCluster: 'microservices-aks'

    namespace: 'orders'

    command: 'apply'

    useConfigurationFile: true

    configuration: 'manifests/orders-deployment.yaml'
```

This provides consistent, scalable deployment to AKS (Azure Kubernetes Service).

Service Discovery and Configuration Management

Services must locate each other reliably. This is often handled through:

- **Kubernetes Services**: DNS-based internal service discovery.
- **Consul or Azure App Configuration**: For centralized configuration and discovery.

Environment-specific variables are managed using variable groups or Azure Key Vault integration:

```
variables:

- group: 'OrdersServiceSecrets'
```

For secrets, use the Azure Key Vault task:

```
- task: AzureKeyVault@2

  inputs:

    azureSubscription: 'MyAzureSub'

    KeyVaultName: 'orders-kv'

    SecretsFilter: '*'

    RunAsPreJob: true
```

Quality Gates and Canary Releases

To ensure production stability, teams often implement:

- **Quality Gates**: Enforce test coverage, code scanning (e.g., SonarQube), and static analysis.

- **Canary Releases**: Gradually roll out to a subset of users.

In Azure DevOps, quality gates can be integrated into release pipelines using pre-deployment conditions and checks:

```
environments:

- name: 'production'

  checks:

  - type: 'Approval'

    approvers:

    - 'admin@company.com'

  - type: 'Invoke REST API'
```

```
inputs:

  url: 'https://gate-service/api/checks'
```

Canary deployments can be done via traffic splitting in Azure Front Door or Kubernetes ingress controllers.

Monitoring Microservices Post-Deployment

Azure Monitor, Application Insights, and Log Analytics provide centralized telemetry:

- **Metrics and Logs**: CPU, memory, custom logs from containers.

- **Distributed Tracing**: Correlate requests across services.

- **Dashboards**: Visualize service health and alerts.

Configure telemetry in the services and send them to Azure Monitor:

```
services.AddApplicationInsightsTelemetry(Configuration["ApplicationI
nsights:InstrumentationKey"]);
```

And enable alerts for failed deployments or high error rates:

```
- task: AzureMonitor@1

  inputs:

    azureSubscription: 'MyAzureSub'

    alertRuleName: 'HighErrorRate'

    condition: 'requests/failed > 5%'

    actionGroupName: 'OpsTeamAlerts'
```

Best Practices Summary

1. **Keep Pipelines Independent**: Allow each microservice to evolve on its own.

2. **Use Templates**: DRY pipeline templates reduce duplication.

3. **Automate Testing and Security**: CI should validate code quality and security.

4. **Embrace Observability**: Invest in monitoring and distributed tracing.

5. **Design for Failure**: Implement retries, circuit breakers, and fallback strategies.

6. **Test in Production**: Use feature flags and progressive delivery techniques.

Conclusion

CI/CD for microservices requires careful orchestration of many moving parts—from independent build and deployment pipelines to monitoring and observability tooling. Azure DevOps offers the tools needed to build resilient, scalable systems. By leveraging YAML pipelines, containerization, and integrated testing and monitoring, teams can confidently ship high-quality microservices in a repeatable, secure, and scalable way.

Legacy System Integration

Integrating CI/CD practices into legacy systems is often one of the most daunting yet rewarding tasks in modern DevOps transformations. Unlike greenfield applications, legacy systems come with technical debt, outdated dependencies, limited automation, and entrenched organizational habits. However, with strategic planning, Azure DevOps can help streamline, modernize, and automate the delivery process for legacy software.

This section covers how to approach CI/CD for legacy systems using Azure DevOps, techniques to reduce friction, and patterns that lead to sustainable modernization.

Understanding the Legacy Landscape

Legacy systems can span multiple generations of technology, including:

- Monolithic codebases written in older languages (e.g., .NET Framework, Java 6, VB6)

- On-premises infrastructure with limited or no cloud integration

- Manual build and deployment processes using shared drives or RDP sessions

- Lack of automated testing or documentation

- Tight coupling to hardware, middleware, or database layers

Before designing pipelines, it's critical to assess:

- **Codebase maturity**: Is the code under source control? Can it be built from scratch?

- **Toolchain dependencies**: What compilers, SDKs, or legacy tools are required?

- **Deployment constraints**: Are deployments performed manually? Are rollback procedures   documented?

- **Test coverage**: Are there automated unit or integration tests?

Answering these questions helps define the scope of what can be automated and what needs to be incrementally modernized.

Source Control and Repository Migration

The first step in modernizing a legacy system is ensuring it is under version control. Azure DevOps supports Git and Team Foundation Version Control (TFVC). For legacy systems still using older version control tools (like SVN or Perforce), migration is often required.

For Git migration:

1. Create   a   new   Azure   DevOps   repository.

2. Migrate the codebase using `git svn` or a third-party tool like `svn2git`.

Example using `git svn`:

```
git svn clone https://svn.example.com/legacy-repo --stdlayout legacy-repo

cd legacy-repo

git remote add origin https://dev.azure.com/org/project/_git/legacy-repo

git push -u origin --all
```

For systems without any version control, initialize a Git repository and add meaningful commit history based on available file versions.

```
git init

git add .

git commit -m "Initial import of legacy application"
```

Once source control is established, other CI/CD capabilities can be layered on top.

Building Legacy Applications

Legacy systems may use proprietary build scripts, batch files, or Visual Studio solutions that target deprecated frameworks. Azure Pipelines can still automate these builds using hosted or self-hosted agents.

Hosted Agents

If the required SDKs or compilers are available on Microsoft-hosted agents (e.g., `windows-latest`), you can use them directly:

```yaml
pool:

  vmImage: 'windows-latest'


steps:

- task: VSBuild@1

  inputs:

    solution: '**\LegacyApp.sln'

    msbuildArgs: '/p:Configuration=Release'

    platform: 'x86'

    configuration: 'Release'
```

Self-Hosted Agents

For dependencies not available on hosted agents, you can install a self-hosted agent on a VM that mimics the legacy environment:

1. Install the Azure Pipelines agent.
2. Register it with your Azure DevOps organization.
3. Use it in your pipeline:

```yaml
pool:
```

```
name: 'LegacyBuildAgent'


steps:

- script: 'build.cmd'

  displayName: 'Run Legacy Build Script'
```

This approach gives full control over the environment and is often necessary for older tech stacks.

Adding Tests to Legacy Code

Legacy code often lacks unit tests. Rather than rewriting large portions of the system, the goal should be incremental improvements:

- Start with **integration tests** around critical workflows.

- Use **code coverage tools** like Coverlet or Visual Studio Test to identify test gaps.

- Gradually refactor to introduce **unit testable components**.

Sample test task using Azure Pipelines:

```
- task: VSTest@2

  inputs:

    testSelector: 'testAssemblies'

    testAssemblyVer2: '**\*Tests.dll'

    searchFolder: '$(System.DefaultWorkingDirectory)'
```

Over time, test automation improves confidence in deployments and enables more aggressive refactoring and modernization.

Automating Deployments for Legacy Systems

Legacy deployments are often manual, involving copying binaries to network shares or RDPing into servers. Azure DevOps can automate much of this, even without containers or cloud-native services.

PowerShell Remoting

You can use PowerShell tasks to perform remote deployments:

```
- task: PowerShell@2

  inputs:

    targetType: 'inline'

    script: |

      Invoke-Command -ComputerName legacy-server `

                    -ScriptBlock    {    Copy-Item    -Path
"\\buildshare\app" -Destination "C:\inetpub\app" -Recurse -Force }
```

WinRM and File Copy

Alternatively, use the Windows Machine File Copy and PowerShell on Target Machines tasks:

```
- task: WindowsMachineFileCopy@2

  inputs:

    SourcePath: '$(Build.ArtifactStagingDirectory)\*'

    MachineNames: 'legacy-server.domain.com'

    AdminUserName: 'admin'

    AdminPassword: '$(password)'

    TargetPath: 'C:\inetpub\legacyapp'


- task: PowerShellOnTargetMachines@3

  inputs:

    Machines: 'legacy-server.domain.com'

    ScriptPath: 'restart-app.ps1'
```

These tools reduce deployment friction and ensure consistent delivery processes.

Introducing Containers to Isolate Legacy Dependencies

When feasible, containerizing parts of a legacy system (e.g., APIs, background workers) can:

- Isolate   runtime   dependencies

- Enable   more   consistent   builds

- Allow   migration   to   Kubernetes   or   App   Services

Even for legacy .NET Framework apps, Windows containers are an option:

```
FROM mcr.microsoft.com/dotnet/framework/runtime:4.8

COPY . /inetpub/wwwroot
```

Then, configure an Azure DevOps pipeline to build and push the image:

```
- task: Docker@2

  inputs:

    containerRegistry: 'LegacyRegistry'

    repository: 'legacy-app'

    command: 'buildAndPush'

    Dockerfile: '**/Dockerfile'

    tags: 'latest'
```

This approach can gradually introduce cloud-native principles into a legacy environment.

Blue-Green and Staged Deployments

Zero-downtime deployments are often a challenge for legacy systems. However, blue-green or canary patterns can be simulated using:

- Separate   staging   environments

- DNS swapping or load balancer reconfiguration
- Manual approval gates in release pipelines

Azure DevOps release pipelines can model this using environments:

```
stages:
- stage: DeployStaging
  jobs:
  - deployment: DeployToStaging
    environment: 'legacy-staging'
    strategy:
      runOnce:
        deploy:
          steps:
            - script: 'deploy-staging.ps1'

- stage: ManualApproval
  dependsOn: DeployStaging
  jobs:
  - job: WaitForApproval
    steps:
    - task: ManualValidation@0
      inputs:
        instructions: 'Please validate staging deployment before promoting to production.'
```

```
- stage: DeployProduction

  dependsOn: ManualApproval

  jobs:

  - deployment: DeployToProduction

    environment: 'legacy-production'

    strategy:

      runOnce:

        deploy:

          steps:

          - script: 'deploy-production.ps1'
```

This introduces safety without overhauling the architecture.

Monitoring and Alerting in Legacy Environments

Legacy systems often lack native observability. Azure DevOps and the wider Azure ecosystem offer multiple strategies to introduce monitoring:

- **Log shipping agents** (e.g., Logstash, Filebeat)

- **Azure Monitor** with custom scripts

- **Application Insights SDK** in supported frameworks

A simple example: pushing logs to Log Analytics with a script task:

```
- task: PowerShell@2

  inputs:

    targetType: 'inline'

    script: |

      $log = Get-Content 'C:\legacyapp\logs\error.log'
```

```
Invoke-WebRequest   -Uri   'https://api.loganalytics.io/logs'   -
Method POST -Body $log
```

This data can be visualized in dashboards, alerts, and integrated into incident workflows.

Gradual Refactoring Strategies

A big-bang rewrite is rarely feasible. Incremental modernization with CI/CD encourages:

- **Strangler Pattern**: Replace functionality piece-by-piece with new services

- **Encapsulation**: Wrap legacy code in APIs or adapters

- **Automated Test Coverage**: Grow a safety net before changing behavior

- **Documentation through Pipelines**: Use pipelines as executable documentation of the system

Refactoring becomes safer and easier when changes are automatically validated and deployed.

Organizational and Cultural Shifts

Beyond the technical work, legacy modernization with CI/CD often requires:

- **Cross-functional collaboration**: Devs, testers, ops must work closely

- **Training and onboarding**: New tools like Azure DevOps need buy-in

- **Pilot projects**: Start small, demonstrate value, then expand

- **Celebrating progress**: Even automating a build or a deployment is a big win

Azure DevOps dashboards, pipeline histories, and boards can be used to show real-time progress and adoption success.

Conclusion

Legacy systems may never become fully modern, but with Azure DevOps and a structured CI/CD approach, they can be transformed into more manageable, reliable, and predictable assets. By automating what you can, containing what you must, and iteratively improving your build and release workflows, even the most outdated systems can become part of a modern delivery pipeline.

Enterprise-Scale DevOps Implementations

Implementing DevOps at an enterprise scale requires much more than configuring pipelines or deploying code to production. It involves a holistic approach to tooling, organizational alignment, governance, and culture. Azure DevOps, with its suite of services—Azure Repos, Pipelines, Boards, Artifacts, and Test Plans—offers a unified platform capable of addressing the complexities of large-scale software delivery.

This section explores key strategies, patterns, and practical configurations for managing CI/CD across multiple teams, projects, and environments within large organizations. It also discusses governance, scalability, and how to align DevOps practices with broader enterprise goals.

Characteristics of Enterprise-Scale DevOps

Before diving into the technical implementation, it's crucial to understand what sets enterprise-scale DevOps apart from team-level efforts. Common characteristics include:

- **Dozens to hundreds of teams and repositories**
- **Multi-region or multi-cloud deployments**
- **Complex compliance and regulatory requirements**
- **Hybrid environments with legacy and modern systems**
- **High-availability, mission-critical workloads**
- **Need for standardization, traceability, and auditability**

The goal of enterprise DevOps is to strike a balance between **autonomy for teams** and **control for the organization**. Azure DevOps enables this through project-level scoping, reusable pipeline templates, policy enforcement, and centralized reporting.

Organizational Structure and Project Hierarchies

Azure DevOps organizations typically follow one of two structural approaches:

1. One Project Per Team or Application

Each team or product owns a separate Azure DevOps project. This model offers:

- Autonomy over pipelines, boards, and repos
- Tailored security and configuration

- Simplified   permission   models

However, it can lead to duplication of configurations and lack of visibility across projects.

2. Single Project for the Entire Enterprise

All teams operate within one Azure DevOps project. This model offers:

- Unified   boards   and   backlogs

- Centralized   security   and   policies

- Easier   reporting   and   tracking

Azure DevOps supports hierarchical area paths and iteration paths to allow individual teams to manage their own backlogs and boards within the shared space.

Example area path structure:

```
EnterpriseProject
├── PlatformTeam
│   ├── APIs
│   └── Infrastructure
├── ProductTeamA
│   ├── MobileApp
│   └── Backend
├── ProductTeamB
```

Scaling CI/CD Pipelines with Templates

To manage dozens or hundreds of pipelines, enterprise teams adopt **YAML templates** for standardization.

Example: Centralized Build Template

```
# templates/build-core.yml
```

```yaml
parameters:

  solution: ''

  buildConfiguration: 'Release'


steps:

- task: VSBuild@1

  inputs:

    solution: ${{ parameters.solution }}

    configuration: ${{ parameters.buildConfiguration }}
```

Teams then include this template in their service-specific pipelines:

```yaml
# orders-service/azure-pipelines.yml

trigger:

  branches:

    include: ['main']


extends:

  template: templates/build-core.yml

  parameters:

    solution: 'OrdersApp.sln'
```

Benefits:

- Ensures all pipelines follow organizational standards
- Reduces duplication and errors

- Simplifies   updates   across   services

Templates can be versioned in a central `DevOps-Templates` repository and imported into team projects using `resources.repository`.

Environment Strategy and Multi-Stage Pipelines

Enterprises deploy to multiple environments—dev, QA, staging, pre-prod, and production. Azure DevOps pipelines can model this through stages, jobs, and environments.

Multi-Stage Example:

```
stages:

- stage: Build

  jobs:

  - job: BuildJob

    steps:

    - task: DotNetCoreCLI@2

      inputs:

        command: 'build'

        projects: '**/*.csproj'


- stage: DeployQA

  dependsOn: Build

  jobs:

  - deployment: DeployToQA

    environment: 'qa'

    strategy:

      runOnce:

        deploy:
```

```
      steps:

      - script: './deploy-qa.sh'


- stage: DeployProd

  dependsOn: DeployQA

  condition: succeeded()

  jobs:

  - deployment: DeployToProd

    environment: 'production'

    strategy:

      runOnce:

        deploy:

          steps:

          - script: './deploy-prod.sh'
```

Environments in Azure DevOps support **approvals**, **checks**, and **auditing**, making them ideal for enterprise scenarios.

Security and Governance

At enterprise scale, DevOps must align with security and compliance mandates. Azure DevOps provides:

Role-Based Access Control (RBAC)

Permissions can be scoped at:

- Organization level (e.g., billing, extensions)
- Project level (e.g., repository access)
- Pipeline level (e.g., approval permissions)

RBAC ensures that only authorized individuals can modify production pipelines or secrets.

Policy Enforcement

Azure Repos supports **branch protection policies**, including:

- Required pull requests
- Code reviewers
- Status checks (e.g., build validation)
- Work item linking

Example policy enforcement setup:

```
policies:
- type: requiredReviewers

  reviewers:

    - name: 'SecurityTeam'
- type: buildValidation

  buildDefinitionId: 123

  queueOnSourceUpdateOnly: true
```

These can be enforced centrally via REST API scripts or the Azure DevOps CLI.

Managing Secrets and Key Vault Integration

Secrets should never be hardcoded in pipeline YAML or stored in plain text. Enterprises integrate Azure Key Vault with Azure Pipelines to fetch secrets securely.

```
- task: AzureKeyVault@2

  inputs:

    azureSubscription: 'EnterpriseSub'

    KeyVaultName: 'SharedSecrets'

    SecretsFilter: 'DbPassword,ApiKey'
```

```
    RunAsPreJob: true
```

This makes secrets available as environment variables without exposing them in logs or code.

Artifact Management and Versioning

Enterprise builds often produce versioned packages—NuGet, npm, Maven, Docker images. Azure Artifacts serves as an internal package repository.

```
- task: DotNetCoreCLI@2

  inputs:

    command: 'pack'

    packagesToPack: '**/*.csproj'


- task: DotNetCoreCLI@2

  inputs:

    command: 'push'

    publishVstsFeed: 'MyEnterpriseFeed'
```

Semantic versioning (SemVer) is encouraged across teams. Pipelines can auto-increment versions using `Build.BuildId` or tags:

```
name:
'$(Build.DefinitionName)_$(Year:yyyy).$(Month).$(DayOfMonth)$(Rev:.r
)'
```

Test Strategy and Quality Gates

Large organizations require rigorous testing to prevent regressions. Azure DevOps supports:

- **Unit and integration tests**
- **UI tests using Selenium or Cypress**

- Load   tests   via   **Azure**   Load   **Testing**
- **Code**   quality   checks   using   **SonarCloud**   or   **ESLint**

Test Publishing Example:

```
- task: VSTest@2
  inputs:
    testSelector: 'testAssemblies'
    testAssemblyVer2: '**\*Tests.dll'
    searchFolder: '$(System.DefaultWorkingDirectory)'

- task: PublishTestResults@2
  inputs:
    testResultsFiles: '**/TestResults.trx'
    testRunTitle: 'Unit Tests'
```

Gates can be configured to enforce quality before promotion to higher environments.

Reporting and Traceability

Executives and program managers often require dashboards to track velocity, quality, and release progress. Azure DevOps provides:

- **Dashboards** for burn-downs, deployments, and issue tracking
- **Analytics** views via Power BI integration
- **End-to-end traceability** between commits, builds, tests, and work items

Example traceability flow:

1. Developer creates a branch and links it to a work item.
2. Pull request triggers build and test pipelines.

3. Build artifacts are associated with the release.

4. Release deployment links back to the originating work item.

This full trace allows compliance audits and root cause analysis during incidents.

DevOps Center of Excellence (CoE)

Many enterprises form a **DevOps Center of Excellence** responsible for:

- Defining best practices

- Maintaining shared pipeline templates

- Curating internal documentation and onboarding guides

- Facilitating training and internal DevOps communities

- Governing security and compliance across projects

The CoE works closely with platform teams to ensure that tooling evolves alongside organizational needs.

Challenges and Mitigations

Challenge	Mitigation Strategy
Tool sprawl across teams	Standardize on Azure DevOps with integrations
Manual deployments in silos	Introduce release gates and promote automation
Poor test coverage	Set coverage thresholds and track with dashboards
Inconsistent pipelines	Enforce template usage with code reviews
Secret leaks	Centralize with Azure Key Vault

Compliance overhead   Automate audit trails via traceability features

Conclusion

Enterprise-scale DevOps with Azure DevOps is a strategic enabler for modern software delivery. By adopting a structured approach to pipeline design, security, governance, and cross-team collaboration, organizations can significantly improve their agility, reliability, and compliance. With reusable templates, centralized secrets, multi-stage environments, and actionable analytics, Azure DevOps scales seamlessly from small teams to global enterprises, making it a robust foundation for DevOps transformation.

Lessons Learned from Industry Leaders

As DevOps practices mature across industries, organizations continue to face and overcome significant challenges in culture, tooling, process, and scale. By studying patterns, decisions, and missteps made by industry leaders, we gain valuable insight into implementing CI/CD more effectively. This section distills key lessons learned from global enterprises that have embraced Azure DevOps as a central pillar in their software delivery transformation.

The insights covered here span financial services, healthcare, government, tech, and manufacturing sectors—demonstrating that while each industry has its nuances, the foundational principles of DevOps remain consistent and transferable.

Lesson 1: Culture Eats Tools for Breakfast

One of the most frequently echoed sentiments from enterprise DevOps transformations is that **tools don't matter if the culture is resistant to change.** Many organizations began their journey by adopting Azure DevOps, only to realize that true progress required a mindset shift.

Key cultural shifts observed:

- **From silos to shared ownership**: Dev, QA, and Ops collaborate around a common pipeline and share accountability.

- **From blame to learning**: Failures in deployments or builds are treated as opportunities to improve, not occasions to assign blame.

- **From big-bang releases to continuous delivery**: Teams release features in smaller, incremental steps, reducing risk and time-to-market.

Microsoft's own journey to DevOps within its Windows and Office divisions emphasized internal evangelism, leadership buy-in, and iterative adoption. By making success visible and aligning performance incentives with DevOps outcomes, they fostered a self-reinforcing cycle of improvement.

Lesson 2: Start Small and Expand

Large-scale enterprises that successfully rolled out Azure DevOps typically began with a **small, focused pilot**. Rather than overhauling all delivery pipelines, they:

- Selected a product team with moderate complexity and a readiness for change

- Introduced automated builds and gated pull requests

- Migrated one environment at a time to CI/CD pipelines

- Documented lessons learned and created a repeatable onboarding template

For example, a major healthcare provider began by transitioning a single .NET application's release process to Azure Pipelines. They reduced deployment time from **4 hours to under 20 minutes**, improved rollback capabilities, and gained visibility into failure causes. Based on that success, the approach was expanded to 25 other services in the next six months.

Lesson 3: Embrace Pipeline as Code Early

Many industry leaders regret not adopting **Pipeline as Code (PaC)** earlier in their journey. YAML pipelines, as opposed to Classic UI-based definitions, offer:

- **Versioning** alongside code in source control

- **Code reviews** and **pull requests** for pipeline changes

- **Templating** and **reuse** across multiple services

- **Greater transparency** and **auditability**

A leading fintech company reported difficulty managing over 400 classic pipelines with inconsistent steps, naming conventions, and deployment procedures. After consolidating into YAML and introducing central templates, they:

- Reduced duplicated steps by 60%

- Standardized environment promotion logic

- Improved onboarding time for new developers

Sample reusable template used across dozens of microservices:

```
# templates/deploy-webapp.yml

parameters:
```

```
    serviceName: ''

    environment: ''

    packagePath: ''


steps:

- task: AzureWebApp@1

  inputs:

    appName:         '${{        parameters.serviceName        }}-${{
parameters.environment }}'

    package: '${{ parameters.packagePath }}'
```

Services then call this template as:

```
extends:

  template: templates/deploy-webapp.yml

  parameters:

    serviceName: 'orders'

    environment: 'staging'

    packagePath: '$(Pipeline.Workspace)/drop/orders.zip'
```

This approach fosters consistency and minimizes cognitive load.

Lesson 4: Automate Security and Compliance Checks

Security is often viewed as a bottleneck in traditional development cycles. Enterprises leading the way in DevOps now embrace **DevSecOps**, where security and compliance are integrated into the CI/CD pipeline itself.

Common techniques:

- Static code analysis using **SonarQube**, **Fortify**, or **WhiteSource**

- Dependency scanning with tools like **OWASP Dependency-Check**

- Pre-deployment approval gates linked to policy checks

- Automated integration with **Azure Policy**, **Key Vault**, and **App Config**

A global insurance company introduced security scanning directly into their pipeline. Example YAML stage:

```
- stage: SecurityScan

  jobs:

  - job: StaticAnalysis

    steps:

    - task: SonarQubePrepare@5

      inputs:

        SonarQube: 'SonarQubeServiceConnection'

        projectKey: 'legacy-api'

    - task: SonarQubeAnalyze@5

    - task: SonarQubePublish@5

      inputs:

        pollingTimeoutSec: '300'
```

By gating releases on quality and security scores, they shifted security left—catching issues earlier and reducing manual review time during audits.

Lesson 5: Decouple Teams with Contracts and Interfaces

Many successful organizations learned that **tight coupling between teams and services** caused bottlenecks in deployment. To overcome this, they invested in clear contracts and APIs, which allowed teams to:

- Build and deploy independently

- Test against mocks or stubs

- Reduce dependencies on other teams for delivery

Azure DevOps facilitated this with **artifact versioning**, **interface tests**, and **contract-driven development** workflows.

For example, an e-commerce retailer implemented the following:

1. Teams publish OpenAPI specs as artifacts.

2. Consumer teams use the spec to generate mocks and begin development in parallel.

3. Upon deployment, integration tests validate the contract.

This model reduces coordination overhead and supports scalability.

Lesson 6: Monitor Everything

Another repeated theme: **if you're not monitoring it, you can't improve it**. Leaders invested heavily in observability tools like:

- Azure   Monitor

- Application   Insights

- Log   Analytics

- Prometheus/Grafana   (for   containerized   workloads)

Dashboards were created not just for operations teams, but also for developers and executives. Examples of tracked metrics:

- Deployment   frequency

- Lead   time   for   changes

- Mean   time   to   restore   (MTTR)

- Change   failure   rate

- Test   pass   rates   and   code   coverage

Sample dashboard setup with Power BI connected to Azure DevOps Analytics:

- **Release   throughput   by   team**

- **Failed** **builds** over time

- **Blocked** **work** **items** and their duration

- **Approval** **bottlenecks** in release pipelines

One government agency created a real-time quality dashboard used during every deployment meeting. This improved accountability and confidence, and it made regressions immediately visible.

Lesson 7: Standardize Without Stifling Innovation

Standardization is essential at scale—but too much rigidity can hinder innovation. Successful enterprises implemented:

- Shared **pipeline** **templates** and **policy** **guidelines**

- **Internal** **developer** **portals** with self-service onboarding

- Governance models that allow **exceptions** **with** **review**

A telco provider, for instance, maintained a central repository of approved build templates, shared tasks, and examples. Teams could fork templates or submit improvements via pull requests. This fostered both alignment and innovation.

They also used pipeline extensibility to introduce custom build and deploy tasks written in PowerShell and Node.js, packaged as internal extensions.

Lesson 8: Empower Teams with Self-Service Environments

Waiting on infrastructure was a major pain point for many teams. Leaders addressed this by investing in:

- **Infrastructure** **as** **Code** **(IaC)** with ARM, Bicep, or Terraform

- **Ephemeral** **environments** created during PR validation

- **Environment** **catalogs** with pre-approved configurations

Example: a team spins up a test environment on every feature branch push using Bicep:

```
- task: AzureCLI@2
  inputs:
    azureSubscription: 'DevOpsSPN'
```

```
    scriptType: 'bash'

    scriptLocation: 'inlineScript'

    inlineScript: |

      az deployment group create \

        --resource-group dev-envs \

        --template-file ./infra/main.bicep \

        --parameters envName='$(Build.SourceBranchName)'
```

These environments are auto-destroyed after the pipeline completes, saving cost and maintaining cleanliness.

Lesson 9: Make Incremental Improvements the Default

Transformation is a journey, not a single migration. Top organizations cultivated a **Kaizen culture**—where small, continuous improvements are celebrated.

Common mechanisms:

- Dedicated time for "pipeline hygiene" and toolchain upgrades

- Retrospectives on failed builds or outages

- Leaderboards for mean-time-to-restore improvements

- Quarterly DevOps health check sessions

For example, a logistics company created a monthly "CI/CD champions" group where engineers from different teams demo pipeline improvements. This led to adoption of containerized builds, caching strategies, and better secret management.

Conclusion

The path to DevOps excellence is neither linear nor universal—but by studying what has worked (and failed) for others, we gain valuable shortcuts and perspective. Azure DevOps, when paired with the right culture and strategic focus, becomes a powerful enabler of continuous improvement at enterprise scale. The lessons shared here reflect years of experimentation and optimization by industry leaders who've successfully navigated the challenges of modern software delivery.

Organizations looking to mature their CI/CD practices should focus not only on tool adoption but on creating a culture that encourages learning, experimentation, and shared ownership—because that's where true transformation begins.

Chapter 10: Future Trends and Emerging Tools

GitHub Actions and Azure Integration

In recent years, the DevOps ecosystem has experienced a significant transformation with the rise of cloud-native practices, automation, and tighter integration between source control and delivery platforms. Among these developments, GitHub Actions has emerged as a powerful tool for continuous integration and continuous deployment (CI/CD), offering seamless workflows directly from your GitHub repositories. This section explores GitHub Actions in-depth, its integration with Azure services, and how to leverage both platforms to streamline and enhance your DevOps pipelines.

Introduction to GitHub Actions

GitHub Actions is a CI/CD platform built into GitHub that allows you to automate, customize, and execute your software development workflows. With GitHub Actions, developers can:

- Trigger workflows on Git events such as push, pull requests, or release tags.

- Define   workflow   steps   using   YAML   files.

- Use   or   create   actions   (reusable   units   of   code).

- Run   jobs   across   different   OS   environments   (Linux,   macOS,   Windows).

The primary benefit is its proximity to the source code, reducing the need to configure external CI tools, and allowing rapid development, testing, and deployment—all from the same interface.

Key Features of GitHub Actions

- **Built-in GitHub integration**: Easily access repo content, pull requests, branches, and commit   metadata.

- **Marketplace**: Thousands of reusable actions for popular tools and services.

- **Matrix builds**: Run tests across multiple environments or dependency combinations.

- **Secrets and environments**: Secure handling of sensitive values and deployment-specific   variables.

- **Self-hosted runners**: Customize environments for more control over builds.

Azure and GitHub: The Strategic Partnership

With Microsoft's acquisition of GitHub, Azure and GitHub have increasingly become more interoperable. Azure DevOps and GitHub now offer several integrations that make it easier to deploy from GitHub to Azure services such as:

- Azure App Service
- Azure Functions
- Azure Kubernetes Service (AKS)
- Azure Static Web Apps
- Azure Virtual Machines
- Azure SQL and other databases

This tight coupling means developers can now choose GitHub Actions as their main CI/CD tool while still leveraging the power of Azure's cloud infrastructure.

Creating a GitHub Actions Workflow to Deploy to Azure

Let's walk through a practical example: deploying a Node.js application to Azure App Service using GitHub Actions.

First, create a new GitHub Actions workflow file under your repository:

```
.github/workflows/deploy-to-azure.yml

name: Build and Deploy to Azure


on:

  push:

    branches:

      - main


jobs:

  build-and-deploy:
```

```
    runs-on: ubuntu-latest


steps:

  - name: Checkout source code

    uses: actions/checkout@v3


  - name: Setup Node.js

    uses: actions/setup-node@v4

    with:

      node-version: '18'


  - name: Install dependencies

    run: npm install


  - name: Run tests

    run: npm test


  - name: Build the app

    run: npm run build


  - name: Deploy to Azure Web App

    uses: azure/webapps-deploy@v2

    with:

      app-name: 'your-app-name'
```

```
      slot-name: 'production'

      publish-profile: ${{ secrets.AZURE_WEBAPP_PUBLISH_PROFILE
}}

      package: '.'
```

Explanation of the Workflow

- **Trigger**: The workflow is triggered on a push to the main branch.
- **Environment**: The job runs on Ubuntu.
- **Steps**:
  - Source code is checked out.
  - Node.js is set up with a specified version.
  - Dependencies are installed.
  - Tests are executed.
  - The app is built.
  - The application is deployed using the Azure Web Apps Deploy action.

To obtain the AZURE_WEBAPP_PUBLISH_PROFILE secret:

1. Go to the Azure Portal.
2. Navigate to your App Service.
3. Click "Get publish profile" and download the file.
4. Open the file and copy its content.
5. Go to your GitHub repo > Settings > Secrets > Actions and add it as a new secret.

More Complex Pipelines: Staging and Production

You can extend the above workflow by using environments in GitHub Actions to separate staging and production deployments. This helps enforce approvals and testing before production releases.

```
    - name: Deploy to Staging

      if: github.ref == 'refs/heads/main'

      uses: azure/webapps-deploy@v2

      with:

        app-name: 'your-app-staging'

        slot-name: 'staging'

        publish-profile: ${{ secrets.AZURE_WEBAPP_STAGING_PROFILE
}}


    - name: Deploy to Production

      if: github.event_name == 'release'

      uses: azure/webapps-deploy@v2

      with:

        app-name: 'your-app-prod'

        slot-name: 'production'

        publish-profile: ${{ secrets.AZURE_WEBAPP_PROD_PROFILE }}
```

Here, production deployment only happens when a release is created, enforcing a more controlled release process.

Using GitHub Actions for Azure Kubernetes Service (AKS)

For containerized applications, GitHub Actions can be used to build Docker images, push them to Azure Container Registry (ACR), and deploy to AKS.

Sample workflow snippet:

```
- name: Log in to Azure

  uses: azure/login@v1

  with:
```

```
    creds: ${{ secrets.AZURE_CREDENTIALS }}


- name: Log in to ACR

  run: az acr login --name myRegistry


- name: Build and push Docker image

  run: |

    docker build -t myRegistry.azurecr.io/my-app:${{ github.sha }} .

    docker push myRegistry.azurecr.io/my-app:${{ github.sha }}


- name: Set up kubeconfig

  run: az aks get-credentials --resource-group myResourceGroup --name
myAKSCluster


- name: Deploy to AKS

  run: |

    kubectl       set      image     deployment/my-app         my-
app=myRegistry.azurecr.io/my-app:${{ github.sha }}
```

This level of automation ensures that every commit can be tested, containerized, and rolled out to a production-like environment in minutes.

Integrating Terraform and Bicep with GitHub Actions

GitHub Actions is also commonly used for Infrastructure as Code (IaC). Developers can write Terraform or Bicep templates to provision infrastructure on Azure and then automate it with GitHub Actions.

Example for Terraform:

```
- name: Terraform Init
```

```
  run: terraform init


- name: Terraform Plan

  run: terraform plan -out=tfplan


- name: Terraform Apply

  run: terraform apply -auto-approve tfplan
```

Secrets for Azure authentication should be stored securely in the GitHub repository's Secrets configuration.

GitHub Actions vs Azure Pipelines

While Azure Pipelines and GitHub Actions both support CI/CD workflows, choosing between them depends on:

Feature	GitHub Actions	Azure Pipelines
Best for	GitHub-native repos	Azure DevOps-based teams
Pricing	Free with limits (more generous for public repos)	Free tier + paid options
Marketplace support	Extensive	Growing
Container support	Yes	Yes
Matrix builds	Yes	Yes

YAML support	Yes	Yes

If you are already using GitHub for source control and want a quick setup, GitHub Actions is ideal. However, for enterprises with deep Azure DevOps usage, Azure Pipelines may provide better alignment with their existing processes and governance.

Security Considerations

- Always store secrets using GitHub Secrets and avoid hardcoding.

- Use environment protection rules for production deployments.

- Enable branch protection rules to control which commits trigger deployments.

- Leverage OpenID Connect (OIDC) integration to authenticate to Azure without storing credentials.

Final Thoughts

GitHub Actions has reshaped how modern development teams approach CI/CD. Its integration with Azure offers a streamlined, developer-first experience that reduces friction from code to cloud. Whether you're building a microservice, a static site, or a production-grade enterprise app, GitHub Actions paired with Azure's infrastructure provides a highly scalable, secure, and efficient path to delivery.

By adopting GitHub Actions, developers benefit from:

- Unified   toolchains

- Simplified   automation

- Improved   developer   experience

- Better   collaboration   and   transparency

In future workflows, we can expect GitHub Actions to further integrate AI-driven tooling, advanced deployment strategies like canary and blue-green, and tighter observability features, solidifying its place at the heart of modern DevOps practices.

AI and Automation in DevOps

Artificial Intelligence (AI) and automation are fundamentally reshaping the landscape of software development and delivery. As DevOps continues to mature, organizations are increasingly embracing intelligent automation to optimize pipelines, enhance security, accelerate time-to-market, and deliver higher-quality software. In this section, we'll explore how AI and automation are applied within CI/CD pipelines, the key tools and technologies, real-world use cases, implementation strategies, and challenges to consider.

The Need for Intelligence in CI/CD

Modern CI/CD pipelines are complex, often spanning multiple tools, services, environments, and compliance requirements. Manual processes—while manageable in small teams—become unsustainable as codebases grow and deployment frequency increases.

AI-powered automation addresses this complexity by enabling:

- Predictive analytics for builds and deployments

- Intelligent test selection and prioritization

- Automated code quality analysis

- Smart incident response

- Behavior-based security monitoring

- Continuous feedback loops and optimization

By offloading routine and repetitive tasks to machines, teams can focus on higher-value work and achieve truly continuous delivery.

Key Areas Where AI Enhances DevOps

1. Predictive Build and Deployment Analysis

AI can identify trends and patterns in build and deployment data. For example, if certain commits or files frequently cause failures, machine learning models can flag high-risk changes early in the pipeline.

Predictive insights allow you to:

- Preemptively fail builds with low probability of success

- Recommend reviewers or approvers based on commit history

- Optimize build agent allocation

This is particularly valuable in large monorepos or distributed systems where builds are costly and time-consuming.

2. Test Optimization and Flaky Test Detection

Not all tests are created equal. AI can:

- Prioritize test cases most likely to catch regressions

- Skip redundant tests when code impact is minimal

- Detect flaky tests that fail inconsistently

This reduces pipeline time while increasing confidence in releases.

Example: Using machine learning to run only relevant tests

```
- name: Run prioritized tests

  run: |

    impacted_files=$(git diff --name-only HEAD~1)

    python select_tests.py $impacted_files > tests_to_run.txt

    pytest -k $(cat tests_to_run.txt)
```

The `select_tests.py` script leverages a model trained on historical data to map file changes to test cases.

3. Smart Code Review and Linting

Automated code review tools powered by AI—like DeepCode or Amazon CodeGuru—go beyond traditional linters. They can:

- Understand code semantics

- Detect security vulnerabilities

- Suggest performance improvements

- Learn from past code changes

These tools integrate directly into pull request workflows, giving developers real-time feedback without human reviewers needing to analyze every line.

4. ChatOps and Intelligent Notifications

AI-enhanced bots can communicate status updates, deployment outcomes, or test results through platforms like Slack, Teams, or Discord. Beyond basic alerts, they can:

- Understand natural language queries (e.g., "What failed in staging yesterday?")

- Recommend actions based on historical resolutions

- Auto-create incident tickets or roll back deployments

This reduces cognitive load on developers and speeds up troubleshooting.

5. Root Cause Analysis and Incident Response

When a pipeline fails or an application crashes, identifying the root cause can be time-consuming. AI accelerates this by:

- Analyzing logs and metrics to suggest likely causes

- Correlating incidents with recent changes

- Identifying common patterns across incidents

Example: Anomaly detection in pipeline logs

```python
from sklearn.ensemble import IsolationForest

import pandas as pd


logs = pd.read_csv('pipeline_logs.csv')

model = IsolationForest(contamination=0.01)

anomalies = model.fit_predict(logs[['duration', 'error_count']])

logs['anomaly'] = anomalies

print(logs[logs['anomaly'] == -1])
```

This Python snippet flags unusual builds based on duration and error metrics.

6. Security and Compliance Automation

AI plays a key role in DevSecOps by automating security checks such as:

- Secret detection in code

- Dependency vulnerability scanning

- Configuration drift analysis

- Role-based anomaly detection

Combined with policy-as-code, this ensures that compliance is enforced consistently and continuously.

Example: Using Azure Security Center with GitHub Actions

```
- name: Check for vulnerabilities

  uses: azure/container-scan@v0

  with:

    image-name: 'myapp:latest'
```

This step scans container images for known CVEs, integrating security directly into the CI/CD workflow.

7. Self-Healing Infrastructure

AI enables self-healing capabilities in deployment environments. For instance, a monitoring system detects unusual memory spikes and automatically scales services, restarts containers, or reverts infrastructure changes.

Platforms like Azure Monitor, Prometheus + Alertmanager, or Dynatrace offer AI-powered root cause analysis and auto-remediation.

Automation Beyond Pipelines

AI and automation extend into other DevOps disciplines:

- **Infrastructure Automation**: Tools like Terraform, Pulumi, and Bicep can be enhanced with policy engines (e.g., Open Policy Agent) to prevent misconfigurations.

- **Release Strategies**: Automated canary releases or blue-green deployments can use traffic data and error rates to determine rollout health.

- **Feedback and Analytics**: Platforms like Azure DevOps Insights or GitHub Advanced Security use AI to provide dashboards and predictive metrics across the SDLC.

Implementing AI in Your CI/CD Process

Adopting AI and automation requires deliberate strategy and cultural shift. Here's a roadmap for implementation:

1. **Instrument Everything**: Begin by collecting metrics, logs, test data, and build history. Data is the foundation of all AI initiatives.

2. **Introduce Automation Gradually**: Start with basic automation like static code analysis or test selection.

3. **Leverage Existing Tools**: Many CI/CD tools already include AI-driven features. Use GitHub's code scanning, Azure Pipelines' test insights, or third-party integrations.

4. **Build Custom Models**: For advanced use cases, use Python, TensorFlow, or Azure Machine Learning to train and deploy your own models.

5. **Secure Your Automation**: Use role-based access, signed workflows, and secret management to maintain security.

6. **Encourage a Feedback Culture**: Use automation to collect and share actionable feedback with developers.

Common Challenges and Considerations

Despite its benefits, AI in DevOps also comes with challenges:

- **Data Quality**: Inaccurate or incomplete data skews model predictions.

- **Explainability**: Developers may distrust AI recommendations without clear explanations.

- **Integration Complexity**: Orchestrating AI into existing workflows can require significant effort.

- **Overreliance on Automation**: Not all decisions should be fully automated—human oversight is still critical, especially in production.

To mitigate these risks, aim for human-in-the-loop systems where AI assists but does not entirely replace human decision-making.

Real-World Use Cases

Case Study 1: Predictive Test Selection at Microsoft

Microsoft uses AI models to select only the most relevant tests for each code commit, reducing test suite time by 80% while maintaining test accuracy. Their approach combines historical data, code coverage, and file dependency analysis.

Case Study 2: AI-Driven Code Review at Amazon

Amazon's CodeGuru provides recommendations on pull requests, helping developers identify bugs and performance issues before merge. It's powered by a decade's worth of internal code data and continuously improves over time.

Case Study 3: Azure DevOps Insights

Azure's integrated analytics and AI capabilities provide release risk predictions, quality trend analysis, and actionable KPIs to guide engineering managers in making informed decisions about pipeline improvements.

The Future of AI in DevOps

Looking ahead, AI and automation in DevOps will continue to evolve with emerging trends:

- **Generative AI for Test and Script Generation**: Tools will write infrastructure code, test cases, or pipeline steps using natural language prompts.

- **Autonomous Pipelines**: Fully self-managing pipelines that adjust in real-time based on performance, security, and business goals.

- **Cognitive Observability**: Advanced AI systems that not only detect issues but understand their context and impact on users.

- **AI-Powered Developer Assistants**: Integrated into IDEs and command lines to offer smart completions, suggestions, and fixes in real-time.

Conclusion

AI and automation are no longer optional in modern DevOps—they are foundational pillars of scalable, reliable, and efficient software delivery. By embracing intelligent automation across the CI/CD lifecycle, teams can reduce toil, detect issues faster, and accelerate innovation. As the tools mature and integrate more seamlessly into everyday workflows, the distinction between manual and automated DevOps will continue to blur, ushering in an era of intelligent, self-optimizing pipelines.

Serverless and Container-First Pipelines

As software systems evolve, DevOps teams are shifting toward architectural paradigms that emphasize scalability, efficiency, and velocity. Two of the most influential trends in this space are **serverless computing** and **container-first development**. Both approaches offer distinctive advantages, and when combined with modern CI/CD practices, they form the foundation for ultra-responsive, cloud-native delivery pipelines.

This section explores serverless and container-first pipelines in-depth, including core concepts, use cases, tooling, deployment strategies, integration with Azure services, and future direction.

Understanding Serverless in CI/CD

Serverless computing abstracts away the infrastructure layer, allowing developers to focus entirely on application logic. The cloud provider manages provisioning, scaling, and maintenance of servers.

In a serverless CI/CD context, applications are typically deployed to services like:

- **Azure**   **Functions**

- **AWS**   **Lambda**

- **Google**   **Cloud**   **Functions**

Benefits of Serverless Pipelines

- **No**   **infrastructure**   **management**

- **Event-driven**   **architecture**

- **Auto-scaling**   **by**   **default**

- **Pay-per-execution**   **pricing**   **model**

- **Reduced**   **time-to-market**

For CI/CD pipelines, this means deploying microservices or event handlers quickly without worrying about runtime environments or server configuration.

Example: Deploying Azure Functions with GitHub Actions

A typical pipeline for serverless deployment might look like this:

```
name: Deploy Azure Function


on:

  push:
```

```yaml
    branches:

      - main


jobs:

  deploy:

    runs-on: ubuntu-latest


    steps:

      - uses: actions/checkout@v3


      - name: Set up Python

        uses: actions/setup-python@v4

        with:

          python-version: '3.10'


      - name: Install dependencies

        run: pip install -r requirements.txt


      - name: Azure Login

        uses: azure/login@v1

        with:

          creds: ${{ secrets.AZURE_CREDENTIALS }}


      - name: Deploy to Azure Function
```

```
uses: Azure/functions-action@v1

with:

  app-name: my-function-app

  package: '.'
```

This pipeline checks out the code, installs dependencies, logs into Azure using OIDC, and deploys the function code package.

Serverless CI/CD Considerations

While powerful, serverless introduces challenges:

- **Cold start latency** for infrequently used functions
- **Observability limitations** without dedicated monitoring tools
- **Vendor lock-in** due to provider-specific APIs and configurations
- **Execution time limits** on long-running processes

To address these, use:

- Azure Application Insights for logging and performance telemetry
- Function warmers or provisioning plans to reduce latency
- Abstractions (e.g., OpenFaaS) to reduce vendor lock-in

Container-First Development and CI/CD

While serverless excels at quick, event-driven workloads, containerization offers a more flexible and portable approach. A **container-first** pipeline treats container images as the primary delivery artifact—ensuring consistency across development, testing, and production.

Tools that support container-first DevOps include:

- **Docker**
- **Kubernetes**
- **Azure Kubernetes Service (AKS)**

- **Azure Container Registry (ACR)**
- **GitHub Actions, Azure Pipelines, and Helm**

The Container Lifecycle in DevOps

1. **Code commit**
2. **Docker image build**
3. **Push to registry**
4. **Deploy to orchestrator (e.g., AKS)**
5. **Monitor and scale**

Sample GitHub Actions Pipeline for AKS

```
name: Build and Deploy to AKS

on:
  push:
    branches:
      - main

jobs:
  build:
    runs-on: ubuntu-latest
    steps:
      - uses: actions/checkout@v3

      - name: Log in to Azure
        uses: azure/login@v1
```

```yaml
    with:

      creds: ${{ secrets.AZURE_CREDENTIALS }}


  - name: Log in to ACR

    run: az acr login --name myRegistry


  - name: Build and Push Docker Image

    run: |

      docker build -t myRegistry.azurecr.io/myapp:${{ github.sha
}} .

      docker push myRegistry.azurecr.io/myapp:${{ github.sha }}


  - name: Set AKS Credentials

    run: az aks get-credentials --name myCluster --resource-group
myRG


  - name: Deploy to AKS

    run: |

      kubectl    set    image    deployment/myapp-deployment
myapp=myRegistry.azurecr.io/myapp:${{ github.sha }}
```

This pipeline builds a Docker image, pushes it to Azure Container Registry, and updates the deployment in AKS.

Infrastructure as Code (IaC) for Container Pipelines

Container-first strategies pair well with Infrastructure as Code tools such as:

- **Terraform**

- **Bicep**

- **Pulumi**

Example: Bicep file to provision an AKS cluster:

```
resource aks 'Microsoft.ContainerService/managedClusters@2023-01-01'
= {
  name: 'myAKSCluster'
  location: resourceGroup().location
  properties: {
    dnsPrefix: 'myaks'
    agentPoolProfiles: [
      {
        name: 'agentpool'
        count: 3
        vmSize: 'Standard_DS2_v2'
        mode: 'System'
      }
    ]
    identity: {
      type: 'SystemAssigned'
    }
  }
}
```

Deploy this template as part of the CI/CD pipeline to spin up infrastructure alongside applications.

Combining Serverless and Containers

Modern systems often combine both paradigms, using containers for long-running processes and serverless functions for lightweight event handlers. This hybrid model allows you to:

- Use serverless for webhook handlers, authentication, file processing
- Use containers for APIs, worker services, batch jobs

Azure makes this seamless with services like:

- **Azure Container Apps** (which supports both containerized microservices and event-driven scale)
- **Logic Apps + Functions** (to build orchestration workflows)
- **Event Grid** (to route messages between components)

Observability in Serverless and Container Pipelines

Monitoring is critical in ephemeral environments. Azure provides several tools:

- **Application Insights** for functions
- **Log Analytics and Container Insights** for AKS
- **Prometheus + Grafana** integration

Example: Instrumenting a Node.js container with Application Insights

```
const appInsights = require("applicationinsights");

appInsights.setup(process.env.APPINSIGHTS_INSTRUMENTATIONKEY).start(
);
```

This sends custom telemetry from within containers, viewable in the Azure Portal.

Canary Deployments and Progressive Delivery

With containers and serverless, advanced deployment strategies become easier to implement:

- **Canary:** Gradually shift traffic to new version

- **Blue-Green**: Maintain two identical environments and switch traffic
- **Shadow Testing**: Mirror traffic to test behavior without impacting users

Tools like Flagger (with AKS + Istio) or Azure Deployment Slots (for App Services) enable this.

Example: Canary release YAML using Flagger

```
apiVersion: flagger.app/v1beta1

kind: Canary

metadata:

  name: myapp

spec:

  targetRef:

    apiVersion: apps/v1

    kind: Deployment

    name: myapp

  service:

    port: 80

  analysis:

    interval: 1m

    threshold: 5

    steps: [10, 20, 50, 100]
```

This example rolls out traffic incrementally while monitoring performance and error rates.

Best Practices for Serverless and Container Pipelines

- **Use minimal base images** to reduce build and attack surface
- **Scan container images** for vulnerabilities before deployment

- **Store images in a private registry** like ACR
- **Implement IaC validation** before provisioning infrastructure
- **Avoid overusing serverless functions** for stateful or compute-heavy tasks
- **Instrument every stage** for observability and feedback loops

Challenges and Trade-Offs

While compelling, these approaches are not without their hurdles:

Challenge	Serverless	Containers
Cold start	Yes	No
Vendor lock-in	High	Low
Portability	Low	High
Learning curve	Low	Moderate
State handling	Difficult	Straightforward
Debugging	Complex	Easier with tools

Successful adoption requires evaluating the needs of each workload and matching the appropriate technology.

Future Outlook

The landscape is shifting rapidly toward:

- **Function containers**: Running serverless functions in containers (e.g., Azure Container Apps)

- **Edge computing**: Serverless and containers running on edge locations

- **WebAssembly (WASM)**: Lightweight runtime for secure, fast deployments

- **Composable applications**: Combining services via APIs, Functions, and containers

CI/CD systems will evolve to support these natively, offering simplified configurations, auto-scaling runners, AI-based optimization, and policy-as-code for all deployment targets.

Conclusion

Serverless and container-first pipelines represent the evolution of DevOps in a cloud-native world. They offer distinct and complementary benefits, enabling teams to deliver faster, reduce infrastructure overhead, and embrace modular architectures. By leveraging the right tools, establishing observability, and following best practices, organizations can future-proof their delivery processes and unlock new levels of agility and innovation.

The Evolving Landscape of CI/CD

The world of Continuous Integration and Continuous Delivery (CI/CD) is rapidly transforming. As development paradigms shift, tools mature, and cloud-native practices become ubiquitous, CI/CD is evolving from a set of scripted pipelines into intelligent, autonomous, and dynamic systems. This evolution is driven by new trends such as GitOps, platform engineering, policy-as-code, ephemeral environments, and AI/ML integration. In this section, we explore the current trajectory of CI/CD, examining how these trends are redefining software delivery and what organizations must do to stay ahead.

From Pipeline-Centric to Platform-Centric Thinking

Traditional CI/CD approaches focus on pipelines—linear sequences of steps tied to specific tools and platforms. While effective, this model often leads to fragmented tooling, duplicated effort, and poor scalability across teams.

Enter **platform engineering**—a discipline that builds and manages self-service internal developer platforms (IDPs) to abstract away infrastructure and delivery complexity. These platforms expose CI/CD capabilities via reusable templates, APIs, and UI portals, enabling developers to deploy code safely without deep infrastructure knowledge.

Features of a modern CI/CD platform:

- **Reusable pipelines and templates**

- **Integrated observability**

- **Automated compliance and policy enforcement**

- **Self-service**   **deployment**   **controls**
- **Support for multiple runtimes (containers, serverless, VMs)**

Example: A reusable GitHub Actions workflow for Node.js services across multiple teams:

```yaml
name: Node.js CI Template

on:
  push:
    branches: [main]

jobs:
  build:
    runs-on: ubuntu-latest
    steps:
      - uses: actions/checkout@v3
      - uses: actions/setup-node@v4
        with:
          node-version: '18'
      - run: npm install
      - run: npm test
      - run: npm run lint
```

This YAML can be included via `workflow_call` across multiple repositories to enforce consistent CI policies.

Rise of GitOps

GitOps is a paradigm that treats Git as the single source of truth for infrastructure and application deployments. Instead of manually triggering deployments, changes to infrastructure or configuration in Git automatically propagate to the runtime environment via continuous reconciliation.

Key principles:

- **Declarative configuration** (e.g., Kubernetes manifests, Terraform modules)

- **Versioned** **and** **immutable** state

- **Automated** **synchronization** between Git and runtime

- **Pull-based** **deployment** **model**

Popular GitOps tools:

- **Flux**

- **Argo** **CD**

- **Jenkins** **X**

- **Spinnaker** **with** **Git** **integration**

Example: GitOps flow using Flux for Kubernetes:

1. Developer pushes manifest changes to Git.

2. Flux detects the change via webhook.

3. Flux reconciles the live state of the cluster to match the desired state in Git.

4. Observability tools confirm deployment success or rollback.

This model promotes transparency, auditability, and rollback ease—key requirements for secure and scalable CI/CD.

Ephemeral Environments

One of the most impactful changes in modern CI/CD is the move to **ephemeral environments**—temporary, on-demand environments spun up automatically for each pull request or feature branch. These environments allow teams to:

- Validate changes in production-like conditions

- Run   end-to-end   and   UI   tests   early

- Enable   faster   feedback   loops

- Demonstrate   features   to   stakeholders

Environments are destroyed after use, reducing cost and complexity.

Tooling includes:

- **Azure Dev Spaces / Azure Container Apps revisions**

- **Kubernetes namespaces per PR**

- **Preview environments in Vercel, Netlify**

- **Terraform + short-lived resources**

Example: Terraform code to provision ephemeral Azure App Service for a PR:

```
resource "azurerm_app_service" "preview" {
  name                 = "preview-${var.pr_number}"
  location             = "West Europe"
  resource_group_name = var.resource_group
  app_service_plan_id = var.plan_id

  site_config {
    always_on = false
  }

  app_settings = {
    "ENV" = "preview"
    "PR"  = var.pr_number
  }
}
```

```
}
```

Integrated into CI/CD, this enables automated provisioning and teardown triggered by PR open/merge events.

Policy as Code and Compliance Automation

As deployment frequency increases, so do compliance and governance concerns. **Policy as Code** (PaC) enforces rules about what is allowed or denied in CI/CD pipelines, infrastructure, and deployments—automatically and consistently.

PaC tools include:

- **Open Policy Agent (OPA)**
- **Azure Policy**
- **HashiCorp Sentinel**
- **Datree (for Kubernetes)**

Example: OPA policy to block deployments on weekends:

```
package deployment


deny[msg] {

  input.request.time.day_of_week == "Saturday"

  msg = "Deployments are not allowed on Saturdays"

}


deny[msg] {

  input.request.time.day_of_week == "Sunday"

  msg = "Deployments are not allowed on Sundays"

}
```

This policy, when integrated with your CI/CD pipeline, stops builds based on time of day, branch, or user role—automating risk mitigation.

Shift-Left Security and Quality

The modern CI/CD pipeline integrates **security and quality checks early**—a practice known as "shift-left". This ensures that issues are identified before they impact production, improving safety and reducing cost.

Shift-left practices include:

- Static Application Security Testing (SAST)

- Software Composition Analysis (SCA)

- Linting and formatting

- Code coverage and mutation testing

- Threat modeling automation

Example GitHub Actions step using CodeQL for code scanning:

```
- name: Initialize CodeQL

  uses: github/codeql-action/init@v2

  with:

    languages: javascript


- name: Perform CodeQL Analysis

  uses: github/codeql-action/analyze@v2
```

Security scanning becomes a natural part of the CI pipeline rather than a manual gate late in the process.

Event-Driven and AI-Enhanced Pipelines

Pipelines are no longer monolithic chains of steps. Instead, they are increasingly becoming **event-driven**, modular workflows that respond to code pushes, deployment completions, metrics changes, or incident triggers.

Combined with **AI/ML models**, pipelines now include:

- Smart test selection

- Predictive build failures

- Automated rollback suggestions

- Self-healing infrastructure

- Adaptive deployment strategies

Example: GitHub Actions pipeline with conditional logic and dynamic matrix:

```
strategy:

  matrix:

    os: [ubuntu-latest, windows-latest]

    include:

      - os: ubuntu-latest

        node: 18

      - os: windows-latest

        node: 16


steps:

  - run: echo "Running on ${{ matrix.os }} with Node ${{ matrix.node }}"
```

These dynamic configurations allow pipelines to adapt to context, reducing runtime and cost.

Tool Consolidation and Integration

One trend reshaping the CI/CD ecosystem is **tool consolidation**. Instead of cobbling together dozens of tools, organizations are embracing integrated platforms that handle source control, CI/CD, observability, and artifact storage in one place.

Examples include:

- GitHub + GitHub Actions + Codespaces + Advanced Security
- Azure DevOps (Repos, Pipelines, Artifacts, Test Plans)
- GitLab (All-in-one DevOps lifecycle)
- Bitbucket + Atlassian stack

This consolidation reduces integration overhead, improves visibility, and enables centralized policy enforcement.

The Role of Developers in Modern CI/CD

In modern environments, developers are not just consumers of CI/CD—they are contributors and designers. Platform teams create the foundation, but developers:

- Write and maintain pipeline templates
- Monitor their own builds and deployments
- Define service-level objectives (SLOs)
- Own the release process via trunk-based development or feature flags

Developer empowerment is at the heart of efficient delivery pipelines. The best CI/CD systems give them control without sacrificing safety.

Looking Ahead: What's Next for CI/CD?

The future of CI/CD is likely to include:

- **CI/CD as a Service with AI Copilots**: Tools that generate, fix, and optimize pipelines automatically
- **WASM-based pipelines**: Faster, more portable CI/CD agents using WebAssembly
- **Edge-native deployments**: CI/CD for distributed and edge networks
- **Explainable CI/CD**: Transparency into pipeline decisions made by AI models
- **Developer Experience (DevEx) focus**: Metrics and tools to improve flow efficiency

These developments aim to make delivery pipelines not only faster and more reliable—but also more intelligent, observable, and adaptable to change.

Conclusion

CI/CD is no longer a set of scripts glued together—it's a dynamic, integrated system at the core of modern software delivery. The evolving landscape demands that teams shift from pipeline-centric thinking to platform-based strategies, embrace automation at every level, and adopt security, quality, and governance as integral parts of the process. By understanding and implementing these emerging trends, organizations can stay competitive, compliant, and innovative in an increasingly fast-paced digital world.

Chapter 11: Appendices

Glossary of Terms

In this section, we provide an extensive glossary of key terms, acronyms, and concepts commonly used in the realm of Continuous Integration (CI), Continuous Delivery (CD), and Azure DevOps. Whether you're a newcomer to DevOps or an experienced engineer looking to brush up on terminology, this glossary serves as a vital reference to support your understanding and implementation of effective DevOps practices.

Agile
A set of principles for software development under which requirements and solutions evolve through collaboration. Agile promotes iterative development, adaptive planning, and early delivery.

Artifact
A file or collection of files generated during a build process that can be deployed to environments. Common examples include binaries, installers, and packages.

Azure **DevOps**
A cloud-based platform by Microsoft offering developer services for supporting the planning, development, delivery, and maintenance of software. It provides features such as boards, repositories, pipelines, test plans, and artifact storage.

Azure **Repos**
A set of version control tools that you can use to manage your code, including Git repositories or Team Foundation Version Control (TFVC).

Azure **Pipelines**
A service that enables you to automatically build and test code projects to make them available to others. It supports continuous integration and continuous delivery (CI/CD) for app development.

Build **Pipeline**
A set of steps that automate the process of assembling and testing code every time a team member commits changes. It includes stages such as compile, test, and package.

CI/CD
An abbreviation for Continuous Integration and Continuous Delivery/Deployment. CI/CD bridges the gaps between development and operations teams by automating the building, testing, and deployment of applications.

Classic **Pipelines**
A GUI-based approach to creating build and release pipelines in Azure DevOps, as opposed to the code-based YAML approach.

Continuous   **Delivery**
An extension of continuous integration that ensures that code can be safely deployed to production at any time. It typically involves automatically deploying every change to a staging or testing environment.

Continuous   **Deployment**
A step beyond continuous delivery in which every change that passes the automated tests is automatically deployed to production.

Continuous   **Integration**
A development practice that requires developers to integrate code into a shared repository several times a day. Each integration is verified by an automated build and test to detect problems early.

Deployment   **Group**
A collection of target machines with agents installed, used for deploying builds in release pipelines.

Environment
A collection of resources that host your deployed application, such as development, staging, or production. Azure DevOps supports the use of multiple environments with approval gates between them.

Infrastructure   **as**   **Code**   **(IaC)**
A process of managing and provisioning computing infrastructure using machine-readable definition files, rather than physical hardware configuration or interactive configuration tools.

Iteration
A time-boxed development cycle in Agile methodologies, typically lasting between one and four weeks.

Multi-Stage   **Pipeline**
A YAML-based pipeline that allows you to define multiple stages (such as build, test, and deploy) in a single file, enhancing modularity and maintainability.

Pull   **Request**   **(PR)**
A method of submitting contributions to a repository. It allows you to inform others about changes you've pushed to a branch in a repository.

Release   **Pipeline**
A pipeline that automates the process of delivering applications to one or more environments. It typically follows the build pipeline and is responsible for deployment.

Repository
A central location in which data is stored and managed. In DevOps, this typically refers to a Git repository containing the source code for an application.

Secret   **Variables**
Sensitive pieces of data, such as passwords or API keys, that are encrypted and stored

securely in Azure DevOps. These can be used in pipelines without exposing them in logs or configuration files.

Self-Hosted **Agent**
An agent that runs on your own machines or infrastructure rather than Microsoft-hosted servers. It gives you more control over the environment and installed tools.

Service **Connection**
A secured connection between Azure DevOps and external services like Azure, DockerHub, GitHub, or other cloud providers.

Sprint
A short, time-boxed period in Agile development during which a team works to complete a set amount of work.

Task
An individual action that is part of a build or release pipeline, such as running a script, publishing an artifact, or copying files.

Template
A reusable file in YAML pipelines that defines a set of steps, jobs, or stages. Templates help promote DRY (Don't Repeat Yourself) principles in pipeline design.

Trigger
An event that starts a pipeline. Triggers can be based on repository events like commits or pull requests, or can be scheduled.

Variable **Group**
A feature in Azure DevOps that allows you to store and manage values that you want to make available across multiple pipelines.

Version **Control**
The practice of tracking and managing changes to software code. Version control systems (VCS) like Git help teams collaborate on development efficiently.

Work **Item**
A record used to track anything you need to track in your project, such as user stories, bugs, tasks, and issues.

YAML **(YAML** **Ain't** **Markup** **Language)**
A human-readable data-serialization language used for configuration files. Azure Pipelines can be defined using YAML to provide a text-based, version-controlled way to configure CI/CD.

Examples of YAML Pipeline Terminology in Context

Below is a sample snippet of a YAML pipeline to showcase how some of the glossary terms apply in practice:

```yaml
trigger:
  branches:
    include:
      - main

variables:
  buildConfiguration: 'Release'

stages:
- stage: Build
  jobs:
  - job: BuildJob
    pool:
      vmImage: 'ubuntu-latest'
    steps:
    - task: UseDotNet@2
      inputs:
        packageType: 'sdk'
        version: '7.x'
    - task: DotNetCoreCLI@2
      inputs:
        command: 'build'
        projects: '**/*.csproj'
        arguments: '--configuration $(buildConfiguration)'
```

In the snippet above:

- `trigger` defines when the pipeline should run, based on commits to the `main` branch.

- `variables` are defined for reuse across the pipeline.

- `stage`, `job`, and `task` organize the pipeline into logical units.

- `pool` specifies the agent used to run the job.

- The `UseDotNet` and `DotNetCoreCLI` tasks perform actions like installing the .NET SDK and building the project.

This glossary will be referenced throughout the appendices and can be consulted whenever you encounter unfamiliar terminology. In practice, understanding this language fluently will make reading logs, debugging pipelines, and communicating with team members far more efficient.

To get the most out of this glossary, consider bookmarking it or printing it for quick reference during hands-on Azure DevOps tasks.

Resources for Further Learning

In the fast-paced world of DevOps, staying updated is critical. Tools, practices, and platforms like Azure DevOps evolve rapidly, making continuous learning essential. This section offers a curated and comprehensive list of resources—books, documentation, tutorials, videos, certifications, forums, newsletters, and more—to help you stay at the forefront of DevOps and CI/CD with Azure.

Official Documentation and Portals

Azure DevOps Documentation
The official Microsoft Azure DevOps documentation should be your first stop. It covers everything from getting started to advanced topics, with deep technical details and regular updates.

- https://learn.microsoft.com/en-us/azure/devops/

Azure **Pipelines** **Documentation**
Dedicated documentation on Azure Pipelines, including both YAML and Classic pipelines. Includes task catalogs, schema references, and examples.

- https://learn.microsoft.com/en-us/azure/devops/pipelines/

Microsoft **Learn**
Microsoft's interactive platform for self-paced learning. Offers comprehensive learning paths with hands-on labs, quizzes, and sandbox environments.

- https://learn.microsoft.com/en-us/training/

DevOps **at** **Microsoft**
A behind-the-scenes look at how Microsoft implements DevOps within its own teams. Useful for understanding real-world scale and best practices.

- https://devblogs.microsoft.com/devops/

Recommended Books

1. **"The DevOps Handbook" by Gene Kim, Jez Humble, Patrick Debois, and John Willis**
   A foundational text that discusses the theory and practice of DevOps culture, tools, and implementation.

2. **"Accelerate" by Nicole Forsgren, Jez Humble, and Gene Kim**
   Provides data-driven insights into what makes high-performing software teams. A must-read for leaders and engineers alike.

3. **"Infrastructure as Code" by Kief Morris**
   Explains how to manage and provision infrastructure using code, automation, and DevOps principles.

4. **"Site Reliability Engineering" by Google Engineers**
   Although not Azure-specific, this book is essential for understanding the intersection of DevOps, SRE, and operational excellence.

5. **"Pro Azure DevOps" by Ovais Mehboob Ahmed Khan and Tarun Arora**
   Focused on implementing real-world CI/CD pipelines using Azure DevOps. Covers both fundamentals and complex scenarios.

Online Courses and Certifications

Microsoft Certifications

1. **AZ-400: Designing and Implementing Microsoft DevOps Solutions**
   Microsoft's official certification for DevOps Engineers. Covers the full scope of Azure DevOps, from planning to delivery.

   o https://learn.microsoft.com/en-us/certifications/devops-engineer/

2. **AZ-104: Microsoft Azure Administrator**
   While not DevOps-specific, this certification provides a solid foundation in Azure services and resource management.

   o https://learn.microsoft.com/en-us/certifications/azure-administrator/

LinkedIn Learning
Search for Azure DevOps and CI/CD-related courses by industry professionals. These are beginner-friendly and offer bite-sized learning.

* https://www.linkedin.com/learning/

Udemy
Udemy features dozens of hands-on courses, including "Azure DevOps: CI/CD using Azure Pipelines" and "Real World DevOps with Azure."

* https://www.udemy.com/

Pluralsight
Renowned for its technical depth, Pluralsight offers specialized tracks on DevOps, Azure Pipelines, Infrastructure as Code, and more.

* https://www.pluralsight.com/

GitHub Repositories and Open Source Projects

Learning by doing is one of the most effective ways to deepen your DevOps expertise. These GitHub projects serve as real-world examples and templates you can use and modify:

Azure DevOps Labs GitHub

* https://github.com/microsoft/azuredevopslabs
  Includes hands-on labs, templates, and examples that align with official Microsoft

training.

Awesome Azure DevOps

- https://github.com/hendrikmuhs/awesome-azure-devops
  A curated list of tools, scripts, extensions, and resources to enhance your Azure DevOps workflows.

DevOps Projects with Terraform

- https://github.com/Azure/terraform
  If you're integrating Azure DevOps with Infrastructure as Code, these repositories offer working Terraform configurations and modules.

Blogs and Newsletters

Microsoft DevOps Blog
Features regular posts on features, updates, and best practices directly from the Azure DevOps product team.

- https://devblogs.microsoft.com/devops/

DevOps Digest
An online magazine providing the latest news, analysis, and best practices in the DevOps world.

- https://devopsdigest.com/

The New Stack
Covers DevOps, cloud-native computing, and CI/CD trends, including Azure DevOps-related topics.

- https://thenewstack.io/

Weekly DevOps Newsletter by DevOps Weekly

- https://www.devopsweekly.com/
  Provides a weekly roundup of tutorials, events, jobs, and tools in the DevOps ecosystem.

Communities and Forums

Stack   **Overflow**
The Azure DevOps tag is one of the most active DevOps communities online. You'll find
solutions to common issues, along with novel use cases.

- https://stackoverflow.com/questions/tagged/azure-devops

Reddit   -   **r/devops**   &   **r/AZURE**
Helpful for candid discussions, tool comparisons, and peer advice.

- https://www.reddit.com/r/devops/

- https://www.reddit.com/r/AZURE/

Tech   **Community**   **by**   **Microsoft**
A more official forum moderated by Microsoft MVPs and engineers. Ideal for structured
discussions and feature feedback.

- https://techcommunity.microsoft.com/

Discord   **Servers**
Look for community-run Discord servers dedicated to DevOps and Azure. These often include
job boards, live discussions, and direct mentorship opportunities.

Podcasts and YouTube Channels

Azure   **DevOps**   **Podcast**
Run by Microsoft MVPs, this podcast features weekly interviews with developers, DevOps
engineers, and program managers.

- https://azuredevopspodcast.clear-measure.com/

The   **DevOps**   **Lab**   **(YouTube)**
A Microsoft Channel featuring deep dives, demos, and Q&A on Azure DevOps tooling.

- https://www.youtube.com/c/MicrosoftDevOps

GitHub   **Universe**   **and**   **Microsoft**   **Ignite**   **Sessions**
Archived talks from two of the most influential cloud/dev conferences. Azure DevOps topics
are frequently featured.

- https://githubuniverse.com/

- https://ignite.microsoft.com/

Example: Setting Up a Learning Plan

To take full advantage of the resources above, consider following a structured learning plan tailored to your current role or aspiration.

Beginner Developer Learning Plan:

1. Complete the Microsoft Learn path for Azure DevOps fundamentals.

2. Follow the hands-on labs from GitHub AzureDevOpsLabs.

3. Watch the DevOps Lab YouTube series on YAML Pipelines.

4. Read the first five chapters of "The DevOps Handbook."

5. Set up a basic CI/CD pipeline using Azure DevOps with GitHub integration.

6. Bookmark the glossary and Stack Overflow tags for reference.

DevOps Engineer (Intermediate to Advanced) Learning Plan:

1. Study for and pass the AZ-400 certification.

2. Learn Infrastructure as Code using Terraform and Azure Pipelines.

3. Subscribe to DevOps Weekly and The New Stack.

4. Contribute to GitHub open-source Azure DevOps extensions.

5. Follow SRE practices from Google's SRE Handbook.

6. Join a Discord server and engage in community-driven projects.

Final Tips for Continued Learning

- **Stay Curious:** Technologies and tools are evolving. Treat DevOps as a journey rather than a destination.

- **Be Hands-On:** Watching and reading can only take you so far. Try deploying a real-world application or automating a project.

- **Teach Others:** Writing blogs, recording tutorials, or mentoring others helps reinforce your own knowledge.

- **Automate Learning:** Set calendar reminders to check the DevOps blog monthly or revisit Microsoft Learn every quarter.

- **Track Your Progress:** Maintain a personal DevOps journal or knowledge base using tools like Notion, Obsidian, or even GitHub Wikis.

By engaging with these resources and building your personal roadmap, you'll stay ahead of the curve and be well-prepared to adapt to the evolving CI/CD and DevOps landscape powered by Azure.

Sample Projects and Code Snippets

One of the best ways to solidify your understanding of CI/CD principles in Azure DevOps is by diving into real-world scenarios. This section includes sample projects and comprehensive code snippets that simulate actual use cases. These examples span from basic CI setups to complex multi-stage deployment pipelines, integrating source control, build, testing, deployment, and infrastructure automation using YAML.

Sample Project 1: Basic CI Pipeline for a .NET Web App

This project showcases how to configure a simple CI pipeline for a .NET web application. It demonstrates how to build, test, and publish artifacts using Azure Pipelines YAML configuration.

Repository Structure:

```
/DotNetWebApp

|-- DotNetWebApp.sln

|-- DotNetWebApp/

    |-- Controllers/

    |-- Views/

    |-- wwwroot/

    |-- DotNetWebApp.csproj
```

```
|-- tests/

    |-- DotNetWebApp.Tests.csproj
```

azure-pipelines.yml

```
trigger:

  branches:

    include:

      - main


pool:

  vmImage: 'windows-latest'


variables:

  buildConfiguration: 'Release'


steps:

- task: UseDotNet@2

  inputs:

    packageType: 'sdk'

    version: '7.x'


- task: DotNetCoreCLI@2

  inputs:

    command: 'restore'
```

```
    projects: '**/*.csproj'


- task: DotNetCoreCLI@2

  inputs:

    command: 'build'

    projects: '**/*.csproj'

    arguments: '--configuration $(buildConfiguration)'


- task: DotNetCoreCLI@2

  inputs:

    command: 'test'

    projects: '**/*.Tests.csproj'


- task: PublishBuildArtifacts@1

  inputs:

    PathtoPublish: '$(Build.ArtifactStagingDirectory)'

    ArtifactName: 'drop'
```

This pipeline builds and tests the project upon any change to the main branch and publishes the build output as an artifact.

Sample Project 2: Multi-Stage CI/CD Pipeline for a Node.js App

This example demonstrates a YAML pipeline that builds, tests, and deploys a Node.js app to Azure App Service using multiple stages.

Project Structure:

```
/NodeWebApp
```

```
|-- app.js

|-- routes/

|-- package.json

|-- tests/

|-- azure-pipelines.yml
```

azure-pipelines.yml

```yaml
trigger:

  branches:

    include:

      - main


variables:

  azureSubscription: 'Service-Connection-Name'

  appName: 'nodewebapp-prod'

  environment: 'Production'


stages:
- stage: Build

  jobs:

  - job: Build

    pool:

      vmImage: 'ubuntu-latest'

    steps:
```

```yaml
    - task: NodeTool@0
      inputs:
        versionSpec: '18.x'
    - script: |
        npm install
        npm run build
      displayName: 'Install Dependencies and Build'
    - task: PublishBuildArtifacts@1
      inputs:
        PathtoPublish: '$(Build.ArtifactStagingDirectory)'
        ArtifactName: 'nodeapp'

- stage: Deploy
  dependsOn: Build
  jobs:
  - deployment: DeployWeb
    environment: $(environment)
    strategy:
      runOnce:
        deploy:
          steps:
            - download: current
              artifact: nodeapp
            - task: AzureWebApp@1
```

```
inputs:

    azureSubscription: $(azureSubscription)

    appType: 'webAppLinux'

    appName: $(appName)

    package: '$(Pipeline.Workspace)/nodeapp'
```

This pipeline defines two stages—Build and Deploy. Artifacts from the build are used in the deployment stage to Azure App Services.

Sample Project 3: Infrastructure as Code with Terraform and Azure DevOps

This sample integrates Infrastructure as Code using Terraform into Azure Pipelines. It provisions an Azure Resource Group and a storage account.

Project Structure:

```
/IaC-Terraform

|-- main.tf

|-- variables.tf

|-- terraform.tfvars

|-- azure-pipelines.yml
```

main.tf

```
provider "azurerm" {

  features = {}

}


resource "azurerm_resource_group" "rg" {
```

```
  name     = var.resource_group_name

  location = var.location

}


resource "azurerm_storage_account" "storage" {

  name                      = var.storage_account_name

  resource_group_name       = azurerm_resource_group.rg.name

  location                  = azurerm_resource_group.rg.location

  account_tier              = "Standard"

  account_replication_type  = "LRS"

}
```

azure-pipelines.yml

```
trigger:

  branches:

    include:

      - main


pool:

  vmImage: 'ubuntu-latest'


variables:

  TF_VAR_resource_group_name: 'devops-iac-rg'

  TF_VAR_location: 'westeurope'
```

```
  TF_VAR_storage_account_name: 'devopsiacstorage'


steps:

- task: TerraformInstaller@1

  inputs:

    terraformVersion: '1.5.5'


- task: TerraformTaskV4@4

  inputs:

    provider: 'azurerm'

    command: 'init'

    workingDirectory:                '$(System.DefaultWorkingDirectory)/IaC-
Terraform'


- task: TerraformTaskV4@4

  inputs:

    provider: 'azurerm'

    command: 'validate'

    workingDirectory:                '$(System.DefaultWorkingDirectory)/IaC-
Terraform'


- task: TerraformTaskV4@4

  inputs:

    provider: 'azurerm'

    command: 'apply'
```

```
    workingDirectory:              '$(System.DefaultWorkingDirectory)/IaC-
Terraform'

    environmentServiceNameAzureRM: 'Terraform-Service-Connection'

    ensureBackend: true

    args: '-auto-approve'
```

This project automates the provisioning of cloud resources using Terraform with secrets and credentials managed through Azure DevOps service connections.

Sample Project 4: Conditional Deployment with Approvals

This sample demonstrates using environment approvals and conditional logic for staging and production deployments.

azure-pipelines.yml

```
trigger:
  branches:
    include:
      - main


stages:
- stage: Build
  jobs:
  - job: BuildJob
    pool:
      vmImage: 'ubuntu-latest'
    steps:
    - script: echo "Building project..."
```

```
      - task: PublishBuildArtifacts@1

        inputs:

          PathtoPublish: '$(Build.ArtifactStagingDirectory)'

          ArtifactName: 'build'


- stage: DeployToStaging

  jobs:

  - deployment: StagingDeployment

    environment: 'staging'

    strategy:

      runOnce:

        deploy:

          steps:

          - script: echo "Deploying to staging..."


- stage: DeployToProduction

  condition: succeeded('DeployToStaging')

  jobs:

  - deployment: ProductionDeployment

    environment: 'production'

    strategy:

      runOnce:

        deploy:

          steps:
```

```
        - script: echo "Deploying to production..."
```

You can configure Azure DevOps Environments to include approval gates for the production environment. This pattern ensures staged rollouts and human validation before going live.

Sample Project 5: Using Templates for Modular Pipelines

Templates help in DRY (Don't Repeat Yourself) principles by allowing reuse across multiple pipelines.

Template File: templates/build.yml

```yaml
parameters:

  - name: buildConfiguration

    type: string

    default: 'Release'


jobs:

- job: BuildJob

  pool:

    vmImage: 'windows-latest'

  steps:

  - task: DotNetCoreCLI@2

    inputs:

      command: 'build'

      projects: '**/*.csproj'

      arguments: '--configuration ${{ parameters.buildConfiguration
}}'
```

Main Pipeline: azure-pipelines.yml

```
trigger:
  branches:
    include:
      - main


stages:
- stage: Build
  jobs:
  - template: templates/build.yml
    parameters:
      buildConfiguration: 'Debug'
```

This modular design allows consistent reuse of pipeline definitions across different projects or branches with varying parameters.

Conclusion and Tips

These projects cover a broad spectrum of real-world use cases, from basic CI to full-stack CI/CD with infrastructure provisioning and secure deployments. Here are some key takeaways:

- **Start simple** and expand pipelines incrementally.

- **Use templates** to modularize pipelines for large codebases.

- **Secure your secrets** using Azure Key Vault integrations and variable groups.

- **Implement approvals** for production environments to ensure controlled releases.

- **Continuously improve** pipeline performance using caching, parallel jobs, and diagnostic logging.

As you build and iterate on your own CI/CD pipelines, refer back to these examples and adapt them for your specific architecture and team structure. Keep your pipelines version-controlled, observable, and always evolving alongside your application.

API Reference Guide

This section provides a comprehensive reference for the Azure DevOps REST APIs and related integration points. Azure DevOps offers powerful APIs that enable you to interact programmatically with nearly every part of your DevOps lifecycle—builds, releases, repositories, pipelines, work items, and more. Whether you're building custom dashboards, integrating with third-party tools, or automating DevOps workflows beyond the portal UI, this guide will equip you with the foundational and advanced knowledge to work effectively with Azure DevOps APIs.

Getting Started with Azure DevOps REST API

Azure DevOps APIs are organized around REST principles. All interactions are made via HTTP requests using standard verbs (GET, POST, PUT, DELETE), and data is typically exchanged in JSON format.

Base URL Format:

```
https://dev.azure.com/{organization}/{project}/_apis/{area}/{resourc
e}?api-version={version}
```

- `organization`: Your Azure DevOps organization name.

- `project`: The name or ID of your project.

- `area`: Service area such as `build`, `release`, `git`, `work`, `pipelines`, etc.

- `resource`: Specific resource like `builds`, `releases`, `repositories`.

- `api-version`: Specifies which version of the API to use.

Authentication Methods:

- **Personal Access Tokens (PAT)**: Recommended for scripting and service-to-service interaction.

- **OAuth 2.0**: Preferred for apps with user-delegated permissions.

- **Azure Active Directory (AAD)** tokens: Used in enterprise integrations.

Example: Curl request using PAT

```
curl -u :<your_pat_token> \

  https://dev.azure.com/myorg/myproject/_apis/build/builds?api-
version=7.1-preview.7
```

Common Headers

- Content-Type: application/json

- Accept: application/json

- Authorization: Basic   BASE64(:PAT)

Example in PowerShell:

```
$pat = "your-pat-here"

$headers = @{

    Authorization         =         ("Basic         {0}"         -f
[Convert]::ToBase64String([Text.Encoding]::ASCII.GetBytes(":$pat")))

    Accept      = "application/json"

}
```

Pipelines API

List Pipelines

```
GET
https://dev.azure.com/{organization}/{project}/_apis/pipelines?api-
version=7.1-preview.1
```

Response:

Returns a list of pipeline definitions with metadata such as name, folder path, and ID.

Run a Pipeline

```
POST
https://dev.azure.com/{organization}/{project}/_apis/pipelines/{pipe
lineId}/runs?api-version=7.1-preview.1
```

Body Example:

```
{

  "resources": {

    "repositories": {

      "self": {

        "refName": "refs/heads/main"

      }

    }

  }

}
```

This triggers a pipeline run using a specified branch.

Get Pipeline Run Status

```
GET
https://dev.azure.com/{organization}/{project}/_apis/pipelines/{pipe
lineId}/runs/{runId}?api-version=7.1-preview.1
```

Returns status, result, and timestamps for a specific pipeline run.

Build API

Get Build Definitions

```
GET
https://dev.azure.com/{organization}/{project}/_apis/build/definitio
ns?api-version=7.1-preview.7
```

Queue a Build

```
POST
https://dev.azure.com/{organization}/{project}/_apis/build/builds?ap
i-version=7.1-preview.7
```

Body Example:

```
{

  "definition": {

    "id": 3

  },

  "sourceBranch": "refs/heads/main"

}
```

Get Build Logs

```
GET
https://dev.azure.com/{organization}/{project}/_apis/build/builds/{b
uildId}/logs?api-version=7.1-preview.2
```

Git Repositories API

List Repositories

```
GET
https://dev.azure.com/{organization}/{project}/_apis/git/repositorie
s?api-version=7.1-preview.1
```

Get Items in a Repository

```
GET
https://dev.azure.com/{organization}/{project}/_apis/git/repositorie
s/{repositoryId}/items?scopePath=/README.md&api-version=7.1-
preview.1
```

Create a Pull Request

```
POST
https://dev.azure.com/{organization}/{project}/_apis/git/repositorie
s/{repositoryId}/pullrequests?api-version=7.1-preview.1
```

Body Example:

```
{

  "sourceRefName": "refs/heads/feature-branch",

  "targetRefName": "refs/heads/main",

  "title": "Feature update",

  "description": "Adding new endpoints",

  "reviewers": []

}
```

Work Items API

Create a Work Item

```
POST
https://dev.azure.com/{organization}/{project}/_apis/wit/workitems/$
Bug?api-version=7.1-preview.3

Content-Type: application/json-patch+json
```

Body Example:

```
[

  {

    "op": "add",

    "path": "/fields/System.Title",

    "value": "Unexpected crash on login"

  },

  {

    "op": "add",

    "path": "/fields/System.AssignedTo",

    "value": "john@domain.com"

  }

]
```

Update a Work Item

```
PATCH
https://dev.azure.com/{organization}/{project}/_apis/wit/workitems/{
id}?api-version=7.1-preview.3

Content-Type: application/json-patch+json
```

Use operations such as `replace`, `remove`, and `add` to update fields.

Query Work Items Using WIQL

```
POST
https://dev.azure.com/{organization}/{project}/_apis/wit/wiql?api-version=7.1-preview.2
```

Body Example:

```
{

  "query": "Select [System.Id], [System.Title], [System.State] From WorkItems Where [System.AssignedTo] = @Me"

}
```

Releases API

List Release Definitions

```
GET
https://vsrm.dev.azure.com/{organization}/{project}/_apis/release/definitions?api-version=7.1-preview.4
```

Create a Release

```
POST
https://vsrm.dev.azure.com/{organization}/{project}/_apis/release/releases?api-version=7.1-preview.4
```

Body Example:

```
{

  "definitionId": 3,

  "description": "Automated release triggered via API",
```

```
"artifacts": [

  {

    "alias": "_MyBuild",

    "instanceReference": {

      "id": "1024",

      "name": "Build_1024"

    }

  }

]

}
```

Permissions and Security API

You can manage permissions, groups, and access levels using Azure DevOps security APIs.

List Users in a Group

```
GET
https://vssps.dev.azure.com/{organization}/_apis/graph/groups/{group
Descriptor}/members?api-version=7.1-preview.1
```

Add User to Group

```
PUT
https://vssps.dev.azure.com/{organization}/_apis/graph/memberships/{
userDescriptor}/{groupDescriptor}?api-version=7.1-preview.1
```

Pagination and Continuation Tokens

Many API responses are paginated. Use the `x-ms-continuationtoken` header to fetch additional pages.

Example response header:

```
x-ms-continuationtoken: "eyJ...ZCJ9"
```

Include this token in your subsequent request to retrieve the next batch of results.

Rate Limiting and Throttling

Azure DevOps imposes rate limits per PAT or token. The following headers are often present:

- `x-ratelimit-limit`
- `x-ratelimit-remaining`
- `x-ratelimit-reset`

Respect these values to avoid request throttling.

SDKs and Client Libraries

While REST API access gives full control, using SDKs is often simpler and safer.

- **.NET SDK:** Microsoft.TeamFoundationServer.Client
- **Node SDK:** azure-devops-node-api
- **Python SDK:** azure-devops

These libraries handle authentication, pagination, serialization, and error handling.

Security Best Practices

- **Do not hardcode PATs** in scripts; use environment variables or Azure Key Vault.
- **Use scopes** when creating PATs to minimize access.

- **Monitor usage** and revoke unused tokens regularly.

- **Leverage Managed Identity** and OAuth where possible for enterprise applications.

Summary

Azure DevOps APIs provide the flexibility to automate, extend, and integrate every aspect of your DevOps lifecycle. From running pipelines, managing repositories, creating work items, to deploying artifacts—every part of your software delivery pipeline is programmatically accessible. By using the examples and references above, you can build powerful integrations, custom dashboards, chatbots, monitoring hooks, and more—tailored to your organization's exact needs.

To go deeper, visit the official API browser: **https://learn.microsoft.com/en-us/rest/api/azure/devops/**

Keep this guide nearby as a reference while scripting, debugging, or integrating Azure DevOps into your custom systems.

Frequently Asked Questions

This section collects and answers the most common questions developers and DevOps professionals ask when working with Azure DevOps, CI/CD pipelines, permissions, integrations, debugging, and best practices. Each question is followed by a detailed, practical answer, often with examples or suggested strategies to address real-world scenarios.

What's the difference between Classic and YAML pipelines?

Classic Pipelines use a visual designer in the Azure DevOps portal. You define pipeline stages and tasks using a drag-and-drop interface. This is great for beginners or for teams that prefer UI-based configuration.

YAML Pipelines are defined as code in `.yml` files, stored alongside your source code in the repository. YAML provides the benefits of version control, reusability, and portability.

Why YAML is preferred for modern pipelines:

- Version-controlled with your codebase.

- Easier to reuse using templates.

- Supports complex logic and conditions.

- Easier   to   review   via   pull   requests.

Migration tip: Use the "View YAML" option in Classic builds to start converting your pipeline.

How can I trigger a pipeline automatically on code push?

To enable continuous integration, define a `trigger` in your YAML:

```
trigger:
  branches:
    include:
      - main
      - dev
```

This runs the pipeline on commits to `main` and `dev`. Use `paths` to narrow the scope:

```
trigger:
  branches:
    include:
      - main
  paths:
    include:
      - src/*
```

Use `pr:` for pull request validation:

```
pr:
  branches:
    include:
```

```
    -  ' * '
```

How do I share variables across multiple pipelines?

Use **Variable Groups** from the Library section in Azure DevOps:

1. Go to Pipelines > Library.

2. Create a new variable group.

3. Add key-value pairs, and mark secrets as sensitive.

In YAML:

```
variables:
- group: SharedVariablesGroup
```

Or reference individual pipeline variables:

```
variables:
  environment: 'staging'
  buildConfiguration: 'Release'
```

You can also pass runtime variables via the UI or REST API.

How do I secure secrets in Azure Pipelines?

Azure DevOps provides several ways to manage secrets securely:

1. **Mark Variables as Secrets**: These are masked in logs.

2. **Use Azure Key Vault:**
   - Create a Key Vault in Azure.

- o Link it to a Variable Group.
- o Enable "Allow access to all pipelines".
- o Reference in your pipeline:

```
variables:
- group: KeyVaultSecretsGroup
```

3. **Environment Variables**: Pass secrets at runtime using secure runtime variables in scripts.

How can I deploy to multiple environments like dev, staging, and prod?

Use **Multi-stage Pipelines** with environments and approvals:

```
stages:
- stage: Dev
  jobs:
    - job: DeployDev
      steps:
        - script: echo "Deploying to Dev"


- stage: Staging
  dependsOn: Dev
  jobs:
    - deployment: StagingDeploy
      environment: 'staging'
      strategy:
```

```
  runOnce:

    deploy:

      steps:

        - script: echo "Deploying to Staging"


- stage: Production

  dependsOn: Staging

  condition: succeeded('Staging')

  jobs:

    - deployment: ProdDeploy

      environment: 'production'

      strategy:

        runOnce:

          deploy:

            steps:

              - script: echo "Deploying to Production"
```

Configure environment-level **approvals and checks** from the Environments tab.

Why is my pipeline not triggering?

Common causes:

- **Trigger not defined**: Make sure `trigger` is specified in the YAML.

- **Wrong branch**: Ensure the commit happens on the branch included in the trigger.

- **Path filters mismatch**: If using `paths`, ensure the committed file matches the filter.

- **YAML file is not in root**: You must reference the YAML path correctly in the pipeline definition.

Use the pipeline run history and the "Run pipeline" UI to test changes manually.

How can I speed up slow builds?

Tips for optimizing build performance:

- **Use caching**: For Node.js, Python, or NuGet packages:

```
- task: Cache@2

  inputs:

    key: 'npm | "$(Agent.OS)" | package-lock.json'

    path: $(Pipeline.Workspace)/.npm
```

- **Parallel jobs**: Use multi-job setups.
- **Reduce pipeline scope**: Use `paths` to trigger builds only on relevant changes.
- **Incremental builds**: Avoid rebuilding static assets unnecessarily.

Also consider using self-hosted agents for heavy workloads.

How do I debug pipeline failures?

Use these steps:

1. **Check logs**: Expand each step in the job. Use verbose output (`--debug`, `-v`, etc.).

2. **Use diagnostic mode**:

```
- script: echo "##vso[task.debug]true"
```

3. **Print** **variables**:

```
- script: printenv
```

4. **Retry with minimal setup**: Comment out non-essential steps and isolate the issue.

5. **Use** **"Download logs"** for offline review or sharing.

Can I reuse pipeline code?

Yes, via **Templates**. Templates allow reuse of jobs, steps, and variables.

Example – templates/build.yml:

```
parameters:
  buildConfig: 'Release'

jobs:
- job: Build
  steps:
    - script: echo "Building using config ${{ parameters.buildConfig }}"
```

Usage:

```
stages:
- stage: Build
  jobs:
  - template: templates/build.yml
    parameters:
```

```
buildConfig: 'Debug'
```

Templates improve consistency and reduce duplication across projects.

How can I integrate third-party services like Slack, Teams, or Jira?

Azure DevOps supports **Service Hooks** and **Marketplace Extensions**.

1. Go to Project Settings > Service Hooks.

2. Choose a service like Slack or Teams.

3. Set triggers (e.g., build completed, PR created).

For Jira Integration:

- Install the "Azure DevOps for Jira" extension.

- Authenticate using OAuth.

- Work items and commit messages can reference Jira issues using `ABC-123`.

For custom integrations, use REST APIs and webhooks to push or pull events.

How do I manage permissions for pipelines?

Use **Security Roles**:

- Project-level roles: Reader, Contributor, Administrator.

- Pipeline-specific roles: Can view, edit, run, delete.

- Environment-level checks: Require approvals or restrict access.

Configure access from:

- Project Settings > Pipelines > Permissions

- Environment > Security

Limit who can access secrets and modify deployment gates.

How can I run pipelines on my own infrastructure?

Use **Self-hosted Agents**:

1. Download the agent from Azure DevOps.

2. Register it to your organization and pool.

3. Install required software (e.g., SDKs, Node.js).

In YAML:

```
pool:
  name: MyPrivateAgentPool
```

Self-hosted agents are ideal for large builds, custom tools, or restricted networks.

Can I deploy to AWS or GCP using Azure DevOps?

Yes. Azure DevOps is cloud-agnostic. You can deploy to any platform using:

- **AWS Toolkit for Azure DevOps**

- **Google Cloud CLI scripts**

- **Terraform for multi-cloud infrastructure**

Example – AWS S3 Upload (inline script):

```
- script: |
    aws s3 cp myfile.txt s3://mybucket/
  env:
    AWS_ACCESS_KEY_ID: $(awsKey)
    AWS_SECRET_ACCESS_KEY: $(awsSecret)
```

Ensure secrets are stored securely using variable groups or Key Vault.

What's the best way to handle feature flags in CI/CD?

Feature Flags let you deploy code without exposing it to users immediately.

Options:

- Use **LaunchDarkly**, **Azure App Configuration**, or custom flag logic.
- Configure per environment:

```
variables:
  featureX: true


- script: |
    if [ "$featureX" = "true" ]; then
      echo "Feature X Enabled"
    fi
```

Flags enable safer releases and faster rollback.

Summary Tips for Common Issues

- **Always commit YAML to source control.**
- **Use separate branches for pipeline experimentation.**
- **Version templates and variable groups for traceability.**
- **Adopt a naming convention for pipelines, stages, and environments.**
- **Schedule pipeline runs using** schedules: **for periodic health checks.**

This FAQ serves as a quick-reference companion for your day-to-day use of Azure DevOps. Keep it bookmarked, and regularly update your practices based on evolving platform capabilities, team feedback, and lessons learned from pipeline usage in real projects.

www.ingramcontent.com/pod-product-compliance
Lightning Source LLC
LaVergne TN
LVHW022333060326
832902LV00022B/4018